IF I WERE YOUNG

CLOVIS G. CHAPPELL

ABINGDON-COKESBURY PRESS

New York • *Nashville*

IF I WERE YOUNG

COPYRIGHT, MCMXLV
BY WHITMORE & STONE

K

PRINTED IN THE UNITED STATES OF AMERICA

To My Good Friends
MR. AND MRS. ROY ARTERBURY
With Affectionate Appreciation

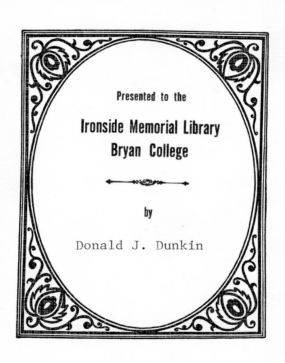

IF I WERE YOUNG

BOOKS BY THE SAME AUTHOR

CONTENTS

CONTENTS

I

I'D FORM GOOD HABITS

"And, as his custom was, he went into the synagogue on the sabbath day."

LUKE 4:16

JESUS WAS A MAN OF GOOD HABITS. HENCE HE WAS A man of good life. Habits make the man. If you are a man of bad habits, you are living a bad life. If you are a man of good habits, you are living a good life. For this reason it is of the highest importance that all of us give earnest and eager attention to the forming of the right kind of habits. This is especially true for those of us whose habits have not yet been fully formed. Therefore I say in all earnestness, If I were young, I would form good habits.

I

Now since right habits are so important, how are we to go about the possessing of such habits? We need to bear in mind that we are not born with certain habits—we make them. How are habits formed? They are the result of our choices. The choices we make day by day gradually harden into

Illus. habits. When a pioneer made his way through the trackless forest, he blazed a trail. That trail was very dim and vague. But by and by another followed his footsteps, then another, then another. Years later that once-dim trail became the Lincoln Highway or some other great artery of traffic. Thus we make choices and persist in them until they become habits.

1. This is true of our wrong choices. When I make a wrong choice, I tend to repeat that choice. It has been well said that it would be easier to find a man who had never sinned than to find one who had never committed the same sin twice. Take the habit of swearing, for instance. No man, I dare say, ever sat down thoughtfully and reached the decision that he would so school his tongue in the irreverent speaking of the name of God that by and by he would be profane automatically and without thinking. Yet many do just *Illus.* that. I was called upon some time ago to minister to a man who was near unto death. He knew of his approaching end. He was entirely rational. I explained to him the way of life, and he seemed with joy to accept it. I believe he did. His loved ones who stood about the bed rejoiced with him. Very soon thereafter the end came. But as he breathed his last breath, his brows puckered into a frown and he went out with a keen oath upon his lips. Of course, he was not conscious. But that oath meant that he had so schooled his tongue in the language of profanity that it had become second nature to him.

Any wrong choice may thus become a habit. We can be guilty of petty insincerities day by day until insincerity becomes native to us. We can be selfish and disagreeable day by day until these habits too become spontaneous. A husband and wife may indulge in petty quarrels with each other till they come to live in the atmosphere of a continuous war whoop. A man may indulge his love of money until the parting with a dollar becomes as painful as the good-by of a mother to a child. A man may indulge in drink until he becomes an utter bondslave.

But it is not only the ugly and vicious choices that harden into habits; it is also true of those choices that are respectable. One may form the habit of refusing to think of God till God ceases to have reality for him. A very intelligent man said some time ago: "As a young man I used to be annoyed by the thought of God. I was not ready to give up my own way for his; so with an effort I put the thought of God out of my mind. Now as I have grown older I have come to feel the need of him, but he is not real to me any more." Godless thinking had become a habit with him.

Some time ago I dealt with a man whose experience was somewhat similar. He was then past seventy. He had known me since my boyhood. He was eager for me to explain to him the way of life. I did my best. I used the method with him that I would have used with a little child. Then we prayed together. When we had risen from our knees, I asked him if he understood. His face was perplexed and wistful. He shook his head sadly, saying, "It seems simple enough. I am sure I ought to understand, but somehow I do not." Then he continued, calling me by my first name, "I am afraid I have waited too long. I am afraid I have waited too long." Godless thinking may become a habit. Thus a man may make wrong choices until those choices harden into habits that become in a profound sense his masters. As a wise man puts it, "He shall be holden with the cords of his sins."

2. Now just as wrong choices issue in wrong habits, so

right choices issue in right habits. Blessed is the man who has made a habit of right thinking across the years. He has built up a reserve of strength that will stand him in good stead in his hour of need. The South Sea Islanders have a conviction that when they slay an enemy the strength of that enemy enters into them and they become strong, not simply with their own strength, but with that of their defeated foe. There is a profound truth in this conviction.

An Old Testament story pictures Samson as encountering a young lion. The story tells us that the Spirit of the Lord came mightily upon him and that he slew the lion. By and by, as he passed that way again, he turned aside to see the carcass of the beast that he had slain. He found that the bees had builded their nests in the carcass; so he came away with his hands full of honey. Thus he propounded the riddle: "Out of the eater came forth meat, and out of the strong came forth sweetness." Thus he became strong with the strength of his defeated foe. Back of the victory that Daniel won by keeping up his practice of prayer when he knew the death sentence would be pronounced against him were daily victories that had made this supreme victory possible. To live a good life, then, we must make right choices day by day; for choices issue in habits.

II

These right choices are to cover the whole business of living. To live well we must have good habits, not in one department of life, but in every department of life.

1. We ought to have good physical habits. If you have been given a weak body, you can vastly strengthen that body and increase your joy in living by forming the right kind of

habits. If you have been gifted with a strong body, you can destroy that body and cloud your daily living with pain and disappointment by forming the wrong kind of habits. Theodore Roosevelt, as a young man, was a bit of a weakling; but he learned how to live physically. He deliberately set about the business of the forming of right bodily habits, with the result that he became a strong man. On the other hand, I saw a young man slip out of life in his early thirties in spite of the fact that he was about the finest physical specimen that I have ever met. He wrecked that magnificent body of his by the most devastating types of dissipation. Generally speaking, to have good health we must have good habits. A friend of mine who had been very diligent in the sowing of wild oats said some time ago, "I have given all that up. This I did, not because I have become religious, but because I grew tired of suffering."

In order to have good physical habits, there must be some routine, some fixed technique about our daily living. We are not to sleep one night and then skip three. We are not to eat every second day. We are not to work all the time and play none of the time. If all work and no play makes Jack a dull boy, all work and no play makes Jack's father a dead man. If you are very strong, you may ignore sensible living habits and get away with it for a while. But nature will charge it up to you and at the last you will have to pay. Many an invalid, by forming good habits, has lived to bury his athletic friend who insisted on doing just as he pleased.

2. If we are going to come to our best educationally, we have to form right habits of study. To help us to do this, we have a certain technique made to order. When we are old enough to go to school, we are enrolled. Having been en-

rolled, we do not expect then and there to receive a diploma. We know that we have only made a beginning. Having entered school, we do not debate each morning whether we shall attend or not attend. We are expected to go five days a week. When we enter college we may be allowed a few cuts, but only a few. If we go to school at haphazard, making a habit of staying out more than of going, of cutting more classes than we attend, we simply do not arrive. We fail to graduate.

If one expects to achieve in the realm of art, the routine is still more exacting. Good study habits are still more necessary. Some years ago we had a couple in our home who were musicians. The wife had to go through her exercises every day. She made such a horrible noise at it that one morning an official of my church who happened to be passing rang the doorbell with utter terror looking out from his eyes. "Who is sick?" he asked. But this method of disturbing the community was a part of her technique. It was the way she was learning to be a singer.

Nobody learns to be an artist in any realm without right habits. You remember the reply that a great painter gave to one who asked him, "How long would it take to learn to draw a circle as you draw it?" The answer was that it took the artist himself forty years. A man who was probably the greatest pianist of our century declared that he had to practice some eight hours a day. He declared further that if he left off practice for one day he could tell the difference. If he left it off for two days, his friends could tell the difference. If he left it off for three days, his audience could tell the difference. In order to achieve our best in school, in the realm of art, in the realm of our daily work, it is necessary to practice until excellence becomes a habit.

3. Now it ought not to surprise us that this same law holds in the realm of religion. How does one become proficient in goodness? There is no magic about it. It is a matter of right choices persisted in until they become right habits. This is not to leave God out. It is rather to give God a chance. Here I think we come to one of our greatest weaknesses as Christians. Too few of us have fixed habits for the practicing of our religion. We have a technique for daily living. We have a technique for the carrying on of our business. But we have no technique for the growth and development of our religious lives.

It has been my privilege to have among my friends some devoted followers of Christian Science. All these without exception had once belonged to some other church. But failing to find satisfaction in the church which they had originally joined, they had turned to Christian Science. Here they were claiming to have found what they had missed and to be living joyfully and abundantly.

How had this come about? What were they doing now that they had not done formerly? The answer in practically every instance is this: In the church of their fathers they had lived without any definite plan. They left all religious practices—prayer, Bible reading, church attendance—to mere caprice. Now they were giving a certain definite part of each day to the reading of the Bible and to the study of *Science and Health, with Key to the Scriptures*. In addition they were attending regularly their public services. The difference between what they are today and what they were yesterday is not that they have found something in their new faith that they could not have found in their own churches. The difference is rather in the fact that they now have a technique for the daily practice of their religion, while formerly they lived at haphazard.

III

What, then, are some of the habits that every one of us ought to form for successful religious living?

1. Everybody ought to form the habit of practicing his private devotions every day. No day ought to be allowed to pass that you do not have a quiet moment for the devotional reading of the Bible and for private prayer. The disciples came to Jesus one day with this request, "Lord, teach us to pray." Prayer is something that we must learn. It is the finest of all the fine arts. We cannot expect to master it in a single day. But as we learn to read the Scriptures, this reading will help us to pray. Prayer will also help us to read the Scriptures wisely and to our upbuilding.

Now in making up your mind to form this habit, do not be discouraged if there are times when you seem to get nowhere. If you can read Latin or work algebra, there were times when the road to your victory seemed quite rugged. There were times when you seemed to make little or no progress. But you did not toss your book aside, saying, "Well, I do not feel like reading Latin anyway." You knew your emotions had nothing to do with the matter in hand. No more must you permit your emotions to deter you from the business of quiet communion with God every day. If you persist, you will win.

2. Everybody ought to form the habit of participating in public worship. When Jesus was a lad of twelve, he went with his parents to worship at Jerusalem. They lost him, you remember, to find him again three days later in the Temple.

When his mother asked him, with a hint of bewilderment and tears in her voice, "My son, why have you behaved like this to us? Here have your father and I been looking for you anxiously!" Jesus answered, "Did you not know I had to be at my Father's house?" In later years, when Jesus had grown to manhood, we read of him this significant sentence: "As his custom was, he went into the synagogue on the sabbath day." Jesus prayed in private. That was a habit with him. Jesus also was accustomed to attend church. This he did not simply as an example. He attended public worship, as he prayed, because of his own need. He could not keep life fit without these two helps.

If we are to live at our best, we must cultivate the habit of public worship. We need the fellowship of those who believe our beliefs and love our loves. We need other high values that come through worship. It was when Isaiah went to worship in the Temple that he saw the Lord high and lifted up. Real worship will bring to us a realization of God. To fail to worship is little by little to lose all sense of His presence.

Not only did Isaiah realize God as he worshiped, but in God's holy presence he became conscious of his own sin. His uncleanness was rebuked in the light of the divine holiness. "I am a man of unclean lips," he sobbed. When he had thus confessed his sin, "then flew one of the seraphims unto me, having a live coal in his hand, which he had taken with the tongs from off the altar: and he laid it upon my mouth, and said, Lo, this hath touched thy lips; and thine iniquity is taken away." Thus through worship this man came, not only to the realization of God and of his own sin, but also to a realization of God's forgiving grace. We can be sure that what worship did for Isaiah in the long ago it will do for us.

3. Everybody ought to cultivate the habit of being helpful to others. One secret of the effectiveness of the Boy Scout movement is its insistence upon each member's doing a good deed every day. No amount of good will, no amount of Bible reading and of church attendance, can take the place of a sincere effort to help others. Many a man who has lost his vision, who is troubled and handicapped by doubts, would be amazed to see how his icy doubts would melt away in the warmth of an effort to do some good in the world.

In order to help others, it is not necessary that we preach to all and sundry that we meet. We certainly ought, however, to be ready to give our personal testimony as opportunity offers. By so doing we would surely find that the word of the Master is true: "It is more blessed to give than to receive." To have the courage to speak to a friend is often to help that friend. It is always to receive even greater help for ourselves. But it is possible so habitually to practice a kindly interest in others that such a practice becomes a habit. We all know those who take an interest in others as naturally as a rose spills out beauty and perfume. These have so constantly loved others as they have loved themselves and have so persistently given expression to that love that it has become second nature with them.

Years ago while traveling in Sweden I was thrilled to meet a man of this kind. Since I was alone I failed to set a definite date for my departure. Therefore, when I suddenly decided to catch the next boat for London, the purser of that vessel told me that there was no berth except in a room with three other men. Though this was not satisfactory, I decided to take it. Now it so happens that I am a bad sailor. Therefore, the ship had not been out of harbor for many hours before I was compelled to go to bed. The bed provided for me was an improvised affair somewhat in the nature of a cooling board. But in spite of the fact that it was far from comfortable, I was getting what comfort out of it I could when a kindly-faced chap looked in and gave me a cheerful greeting. "How are you coming?" he asked.

"Finely!" I answered out of my abundant agony.

He then stepped across the room to tuck in my covers. Discovering what sort of bed I had, he said to me almost sternly, "This is my bed."

"No," I replied, "it is not, but it isn't comfortable enough to argue about. Besides I am not in an argumentative frame of mind. I am traveling for pleasure, so leave me to my enjoyment."

At that he went away. Night came, and I decided to go up on deck. This I did. Having attended to a few chores up there, I was driven back to bed again. But when I reached our room, I found that my afternoon visitor had taken my bed. There he lay pretending to be asleep—I do not know whether he was or not. I had perforce to take his bed, which was as comfortable as mine was uncomfortable.

"Why did he do that?" I said to myself as I looked at him in the twilight of that northern light. Usually men who are not selfish at any other time are selfish when they are traveling. But here was a man whose face I had never seen till today, yet he was doing me a favor in spite of myself. Of course, I sought him out the next morning to express my gratitude and to ask him why he did it. He was a Britisher and seemed decidedly embarrassed by my gratitude. He also seemed reluctant to tell me anything about himself. At last he said, "I have been doing a bit of missionary work over in the Congo for the last ten years. I am coming home on a furlough. I saw that you were ill and that your bed was uncomfortable. I knew you would not accept mine unless you had to. I hope you will pardon me." So long had he forgotten himself by remembering others that it had become a beautiful habit. Blessed, therefore, is the man who forms good habits; for good habits mean a good life.

I'D MIND MY OWN BUSINESS

*"And as thy servant was busy here and there, he was
gone."*

I KINGS 20:40

HIS IS A PART OF AN OLD TESTAMENT PARABLE. A CER-
tain notable prisoner has been captured. His safekeeping
is of the highest importance. Therefore, a particular soldier
has been singled out from all his fellows to perform this task.
Naturally this soldier should feel honored in being so trusted.
But if his is a great honor, his is also a great responsibility.
So important is his task that he is warned that, if the prisoner
is allowed to escape, an unpayable fine will be assessed against
him or his own life will have to be given for that of his
prisoner.

How does this honored and trusted soldier respond? He
fails to measure up. When he is asked for his prisoner, he
cannot deliver. The man on whose safekeeping so much depended, even to the life of the man set to guard him, has been
allowed to escape. This was the case not because the guard
was overpowered, not because the task was impossible. He

was allowed to escape rather because the man honored with this weighty responsibility did not have time to discharge it. "While thy servant was busy here and there, he was gone."

Now this old story has something very definite to say to every one of us. It speaks in a peculiar fashion to you who are in life's green spring. It has a very personal message to all of you who have not yet found yourselves and have not yet fully decided how you will use your lives. There are three definite facts about this man to which I wish to call your attention.

I

The first fact is that this man of the long ago had a particular task assigned to him. He was set free from all other tasks that he might give himself solely to the doing of this one thing. He had a business that was his very own. Now what was true of him is, I take it, true of every one of us. You have perhaps heard of the small boy who was accustomed to carry a written excuse to his teacher when for some reason he had to miss a day from school or had to be late. One day the teacher asked him to bring his birth certificate when he came to school next day. But the lad forgot it. Therefore, when he reached school, he hurried to his teacher to tell her, "I forgot my excuse for being born." Well, that is a type of forgetfulness that is all too common.

But even though we forget, I am convinced that God has a purpose for every life, that he gives to every man his work. I find it easy to believe this because everywhere we look in our wonderful universe we see marks of intelligent planning. This is true from the most minute that we can see through the microscope to the most tremendous that we see through the telescope. With the psalmist we can hear the heavens declaring the glory of God. We can sing with Addison as we look at the distant stars,

> "In reason's ear they all rejoice,
>   And utter forth a glorious voice;
>   Forever singing, as they shine,
>   'The hand that made us is divine.'"

We can read God's guidance in the flight of the bird from its wintry home to the land of summer. And as we thus see the marks of plan and purpose in the animate and inanimate, we can believe that the God who planned the lesser will plan that which is of supreme worth—your life and mine. We can believe with Bryant, as he watches the bird of passage on its sure course, that

> "He who, from zone to zone,
> Guides through the boundless sky thy certain flight,
> In the long way that I must tread alone,
>   Will lead my steps aright."

Then we can believe that God has a definite task for every one of us because that is the clear teaching of his word. We read it in the Old Testament. One day the word of the Lord came to Jeremiah, telling him to go down to the potter's house, where he would hear God's word. When the prophet in obedience to this command entered into that ancient manufacturing establishment three objects at once caught his eye. First there was the potter; then the wheel, that with which the potter worked; then the plastic clay, that upon which the potter worked. As the prophet looked on, he saw the clay, shapeless and ugly. But he realized that there was a place where this clay was no longer ugly but beautiful, no longer a bit of plastic prose but of winsome poetry. Where was that? It was in the mind of the potter. The potter was not working at random. He was working according to plan. "Then the word of the Lord came to me, saying . . . As the clay is in the potter's hand, so are ye in mine hand, O house of Israel."

This same teaching becomes, if possible, even more emphatic in the New Testament. There is nothing more evident than that the life of Jesus was lived, not according to his own plan and purpose, but according to the plan and purpose of God. He emphasizes this fact again and again. "My meat," he declares, "is to do the will of him that sent me, and to finish his work." He was constantly undergirded by a sense of mission. But he is sure that God no more planned his own life than he plans yours and mine. As he gave to Jesus his work, so he gives a particular task to you and me. "As my Father hath sent me, even so send I you."

Then the Bible teaches this also through personalities that walk across its pages. "David, after he had served his own generation by the will of God, fell on sleep, and was laid unto his fathers." That is, David's life was strong and useful just in proportion as he minded his own business by carrying out the will of God in his own life. Saul, on the other hand, while a man free from some of the vices that marred the life of David, missed his great opportunity. By refusing to do the will of God, he refused to enter into God's plan and purpose for him. Thus he threw himself away. Men and nations as they appear on the pages of the Bible come to usefulness and victory or to uselessness and defeat in proportion as they are loyal to the will of God. We may, therefore, believe that as this man of the long ago had a particular task to perform, the same is true of you and me.

II

Not only did this man have a particular task, but he knew what that task was. This, I take it, is also your privilege and mine. In spite of the fact that we are often very uncertain, in spite of the fact that some of us never seem to find our places in the scheme of things, I believe that it is possible for every one to know his own business. By this I do not mean that God will give us once and for all a blueprint of every turn of the road. But I do believe that he will enable us to look up from our task and say with conviction, "To this end was I born, and for this cause came I into the world."

How, then, may we come to know our business? The first step, I take it, is a definite dedication to God. It is every man's highest obligation and highest privilege to be a follower of Jesus Christ. It is every man's full duty to put himself and the best that he knows into God's hands. "Yield yourselves unto God." That is a call that comes to every human soul. It is the very least that we can do and be Christian. It is the most that we can do either in time or in eternity. Our first business is to dedicate our lives to God.

To those who thus dedicate themselves God promises his definite guidance. "In all thy ways acknowledge him, and he shall direct thy paths." He will not guide all of us in the same fashion. To some he will speak through the voice of need. These will hear his call in opportunities for service. Others will be guided in part through the counsel of consecrated friends. Then I believe God guides us through our tastes and through our aptitudes. Other things being equal,

I believe God calls us to do the things that we can do and the thing that we long to do. We can go further following our own bent and aptitudes than we can against them.

Then God guides through our sanctified common sense. Our own intelligence tells us that our contribution, whatever its nature, is to be active and not merely passive. God calls us to have a part in the game and not merely to sit on the side line. There are literally thousands of people all about us who are in sympathy with the Church, who believe in the supreme worth of its mission, but who for some reason hold themselves aloof. These are not minding their own business. It is every man's solemn obligation to make an active and aggressive effort toward the building of a better world.

Not only are we to have an active part in doing what needs to be done, but we are to work constructively. Whatever may be your business in life, it is not to tear down but to build up. When Mary made her priceless contribution at the feast in the house of Simon the leper, what part did Judas play? The part of the destructive critic. Believe me, it takes less heart and less brains to tear down, to destroy, than to do almost anything else in the world. Your business and mine, whatever its nature, is constructive and not destructive.

Then finally, plain common sense tells us that our business is co-operative. When I say I am going to mind my own business, that sounds to some very narrow. It sounds as if I were an isolationist. But such is not the case. I cannot mind my own business without taking an interest in my neighbor. I cannot mind my own business without taking an interest in the wide world. Some years ago when I asked a father to make a contribution to some orphan children, he answered that he had an orphan of his own. He was saying, "I have a child of my own to look after. That child is my business. Other children are not my business."

But his common sense would have told him, had he been willing to listen, that his position was utterly false. That child of his might have to play with those other children. He might later marry one of them. Therefore, they were his business. In fact, no man can be intelligently interested in the smallest child without being interested in his city, in the schools of that city, in the churches of that city, in the theaters of that city. He cannot be intelligently interested in the smallest child without being interested in his nation and in his world. If the nations of the earth are not Christianized, a sudden Pearl Harbor may break upon the world and that child whom he has taught to love peace may be forced into war. As individuals and as nations, minding our own business has to do with duties close at hand. It also has concerns as wide as the world.

It so happens that I am a Christian minister. My business is the proclamation of the gospel. That task is not narrow. It is as wide as the needs of mankind. Often when a minister discusses some social evil such as right working conditions, war, the liquor traffic, there is a protest from the pew and a call for the old-time gospel. I remember still with what fervor certain newspapers and wet politicians tried to scourge the ministers back into their pulpits during the Prohibition campaign of 1928. The preacher was urged with vehemence and passion to mind his own business. But it so happens that humanity is his business. If that is not the case, then the priest and the Levite that passed that dying man on the roadside were not guilty. They were merely minding their own business.

This, then, is true of all of us: It is our business to do the will of God, to work actively, constructively, and co-operatively for the good of mankind. But more than this is promised. If we give God a chance, he will give us definite guidance, though we may not always be keenly conscious of it at the time. There is a kindly Light that leads amid the encircling gloom. As most of us who are Christians look back upon our yesterdays, there are not many decisions that we would change. Some of the churches that I have served I would never have served had it been left to my own choice. Yet I realize now that every one of these made a definite contribution to me personally, however little I may have contributed to them. I think almost all of us can go as far as Shakespeare and say,

> "There's a divinity that shapes our ends,
>   Rough-hew them how we will."

We have a business and it is our privilege to know what that business is.

III

The final word about this man is that he failed to mind his business. This he did not because his task was impossible. This he did not because his assignment made him bitter and resentful. No more did he fail because he was a deliberate traitor to his country. Neither did he go wrong because he accepted a bribe for the release of his prisoner. He simply got so busy minding the business of somebody else that he forgot his own. "And as thy servant was busy here and there, he was gone."

Now it is our privilege to go right where he went wrong. If I were young, I would mind my own business for the following reasons:

1. I would mind my own business because that is the one big thing that I can do. There are many worthful tasks that appeal to me. How often I have wished that I could preach as well as some brilliant brother minister! How often I have longed to sing like some gifted artist! But while these prizes are beyond my reach, there is one prize, the biggest and the best, that I can make my very own. I can mind my own business. I can carry out God's purpose and plan in my life. Certainly I cannot do everything, but I can do this one thing—I can mind my own business. This I can do in spite of man or devils. If you mind your business, it will help me to mind mine. But I can still mind mine even if you fail. Every man can mind his own business.

2. If I were young, I would mind my own business because this is my greatest privilege. First, it is a privilege because such a course is a great safeguard against spiritual and physical sickness. How many people turn aside every day to ways of evil simply because they lack a bracing sense of mission! They go to the devil for the lack of anything better to do.

Then as minding one's own business is conducive to spiritual health, so it is to health of mind and body. I think it would amaze us to realize how many people are sick both mentally and physically for lack of anything else to do. I am thinking now of a woman whom I know well. She is genuinely in earnest and fancies that she is deeply religious. But for years she has been spoiled and petted. For years she has had nothing to do except to feel her own pulse, look at her own tongue, and give a blow-by-blow description of the way her nerves are acting. This has gone on so long that I am quite sure that were she to wake tomorrow morning as strong as Joe Louis, she would still pity herself for being such a hopeless invalid. Certainly one secret of her sickness is that she has nothing else to do.

Then another benefit of minding our own business is that it is a safeguard against interfering in the business of others. Few of us love meddlers. But why do we meddle? Why do we often engage in critical gossip? Why do we spend so much time discussing what Tom, Dick, and Harry ought to do? How is it that we know so well just what everybody else ought to do? Why is it we so often meddle in their business with our tongues if not with our hands? One big reason is that we are refusing to mind our own business.

Finally, to mind one's own business is a great privilege because it is the one way we can guarantee to ourselves the uplifting and undergirding presence of God. One seductive word that the tempter spoke to Jesus was this: having set him upon a pinnacle of the temple, he said: "If thou be the Son of God, cast thyself down from hence: for it is written, He shall give his angels charge over thee, to keep thee: and in their hands they shall bear thee up, lest at any time thou dash thy foot against a stone." But you will notice that the tempter left out one significant word. That was this—"In all thy ways." What he is suggesting to the Master is, "Go your own way. God will keep you whether you are within his will or not." But such is not the case. We have no promise of God's keeping when we take ourselves out of his hands and do as we please. But as long as we mind our own business, nothing can harm us. He will indeed keep us in all our ways. Thus to mind one's own business is to have the undergirding presence of God.

3. If I were young, I would mind my own business because to fail to do this, however much I might attain elsewhere, would be to make a tragedy of life. Just what this man of the long ago accomplished by being busy here and there we do not know. In fact, it does not matter. The one tragic fact is that by being busy here and there he failed to mind his own business. His was the sin of neglect. It was this that caused him to have to face a firing squad. To neglect any business is surely to destroy that business. The best man in our village when I was a boy was its leading merchant. He had a host of friends who were eager to trade with him. But his business went into the hands of the receiver through his own neglect. To neglect one's business ends in tragedy.

On the other hand, to mind one's business means victory however many other tasks we may have failed to accomplish. When Jesus reached the end of the way, he certainly did not look like a success in the eyes of the world. Yet as he stood under the shadow of the cross, he declared: "I have glorified thee on the earth: I have finished the work which thou gavest me to do." By this he was simply saying, "I have lived within thy will. I have minded my own business." Thus living, he had reached perfection. That is all that is asked of you and me. We are not asked to give so much money, to reach so many men, to attain certain ends. All we are asked to do is to live day by day within the will of God. How that simplifies life! Will you begin it now? Will you purpose to continue it until you see him face to face and hear his "Well done!"

I'D MEET LIFE'S REQUIREMENTS

"I must . . ."

JOHN 9:4

WE ENTER THE SCHOOL OF LIFE WITHOUT OUR CONSENT. As another has said, "our little spoonful of existence is measured out to us and no questions asked." I think most of us, had we been consulted, would have chosen to enter this school in spite of its difficulties. Naturally, there are some exceptions. It became the fashion a few years ago for some ultramodern youngsters to remind their parents of the fact that they did not ask to be born. Of course, they were speaking sober truth. Their parents might have spoken with equal truthfulness by reminding them that they would not have asked them to be born had they known that they were going to be such graceless nitwits. But whether willingly or unwillingly, we have all been entered in this school of life.

Not only do we find ourselves in this school, but we are confronted by certain courses that are required. That is true of every one of us. Jesus himself was no exception. "I must," he said again and again. That same word certainly befits our lips. To be sure, there are some very inviting electives open to us. But this is by no means true of all the courses that are offered. I have known a few educators who believed that all courses ought to be matters of choice. Whether in so thinking they were wise or not I cannot say. But this fact I can affirm with certainty: God does not run his school in that fashion. There are courses that he requires regardless of the aptitude or taste or willingness of the individual. To face this fact, therefore, is a matter of plain common sense.

I

What are some of these courses that are required?

1. There are requirements that grow out of our physical needs. Whatever may be our attitude, for instance, toward food, all of us must eat. There is a wide latitude of choice as to what we shall eat and when and how much, but eat we must. That is not an elective; it is a requirement. The same is true of sleep. Some may choose to sleep too much; some may choose to sleep too little. Some energetic souls may prefer not to sleep at all. But however energetic we may be, we have to sleep. Nature sooner or later will close our eyes in sleep even though the penalty for such sleep might be death. There are some needs of the body, therefore, that are requirements.

2. A second requirement is temptation. Some may be indifferent to temptation. Others may resent it. But whatever our attitude, no single one can avoid it. Temptation is an absolutely universal experience. Of course, there are ways that we can diminish or increase our temptations. We can also diminish or increase our chances of victory. But there is no way we can escape temptation altogether. We cannot

escape, for instance, through a wholesome environment. A good environment can greatly lessen our temptations. The child born into the wholesome atmosphere of an old-fashioned country home such as I knew as a boy has a far better chance than the child of the slums. Yet even the best of environments cannot give us complete exemption. The wise writer of the book of Genesis emphasizes this fact when he pictures the first temptation as taking place in a garden so close to heaven that God came to walk in it in the cool of the day.

It is a great help toward resisting temptation to be well born. Happy is the youth that has flowing in his veins the moral momentum of a clean and pious ancestry. By our own failures and follies we can handicap our children. It is possible for us to stand at the upstairs window of life and pour the acid of weakness into the faces of our oncoming boys and girls. It is also possible for us to share with them our strength. But there is no possible way of saving them from temptation altogether. This, too, the author of Genesis emphasizes by showing us man falling into temptation though fresh and clean from the hand of God.

Then we can lessen our temptations by the winning of the small battles of life's commonplace days. There is little doubt that the supreme treachery of Judas at the end of his journey was but the sum total of the petty treacheries of his ordinary days. When Daniel opened his window toward Jerusalem and prayed in spite of the king's decree, he was but giving expression in one great test of loyalty to the smaller victories of his yesterdays. But while our moral victories can help, they cannot exempt. Jesus never lost a battle. Yet that fact did not exempt him from temptation. "He was in all points

34

tempted like as we are," says the writer to the Hebrews, "yet without sin." Temptation, then, is not an elective but a requirement.

This is just another way of saying that we live our lives in a realm of choices. We have to listen every day to the upward call and to the call that leads downward. Every day we stand at the forks of the road and must choose the one way or the other. This means conflict, struggle. The fact that temptation is universal means that life is a battle. There are those that seem to refuse to fight. They seem to insist always on the easy road. Yet I am persuaded that even the flimsiest failures put up some bit of a fight. We see the failure, but we fail to see the conflict that went before. Temptation and conflict, then, are experiences of all of us.

3. A third requirement is judgment. Our fathers used to preach rather lurid sermons about the judgment to come. We have far less to say about the judgment that we are to face on life's other side, but we have far more to say about the judgments that we experience in the here and now. We have just said that temptation is a universal experience. Every man is tempted. Every man must also face the results of his temptation. Every man must reap according to his sowing. This does not mean, of course, that God pays off at the close of each day or even every Saturday night. If we thus reaped in exact mathematical fashion, a man would deserve no more credit for his right choices than a hireling for working for his wages. But no individual, no nation, gets away with anything. Judgment is a requirement in life's school.

4. The fourth requirement I mention is change. There are those who revel in change. They like to push about the

furniture in their homes. They like to push their fellows about. They would have the sun rising in the west instead of the east if they could, just for the sake of variety. But while there are some who delight in change, there are far more who hate it. There are those who have dropped into comfortable ruts mentally, spiritually, and otherwise, from which they are loath to be shaken. There are those who, consciously or unconsciously, long for a static world and even for a static God. But this is impossible. Whether we like it or dislike it, change is a universal law of life. We ourselves, our loved ones, our world, are in a constant flux. Change is a required course.

5. Finally, suffering is one of life's requirements. It has been well said that life begins with the pain of birth and ends in the pain of death. Between the two events there is a strange mingling of sunshine and shadow, of laughter and tears. This is not to deny that much of our suffering comes as a result of the follies and failures and sins of ourselves and of others. But when all this is taken into account, there are tragedies that we cannot fully explain. There are sorrows in life against which we must press our aching and bleeding hearts, shrink from them how we may. Sooner or later to all of us, however sheltered, comes the experience of pain.

II

What are we, as pupils in the school of life, to do with these requirements?

1. There are those who flunk the course by seeking to be exceptions to the rule. They decide that these are required subjects for everybody except themselves. For instance, everybody has to eat. It seems there would not be a dissenting

voice to that. Yet I knew a minister personally a few years ago who made up his mind that he would be clothed with the Godhead bodily. He sought to do this by refusing to eat. He was a strong, husky chap; but he became a wizened and ghastly creature. Of course, he was not clothed with the Godhead bodily. On the contrary, he would have been clothed with his own shroud had not his physician hurried him to the hospital and saved him by forced feeding after he had fallen in a coma as the result of his long fasting.

Since there are those who fancy themselves exceptions to the rule that all must eat, we need not be surprised to find those who persuade themselves that the law of sowing and reaping operates for the other fellow but not for them. Silly souls may allow their sins to find them out, but they themselves are far too shrewd for that! They are sure that they have developed sufficient cunning to reverse the laws of nature and to gather grapes of thorns and figs of thistles. That was Jezebel's conviction. It has been the conviction of many another. When Jehu, you remember, came to Jezreel in search of that cruel and brilliant woman, she did not hide. She rather dressed her hair and painted her face and posted herself at the window to preach this soldier a sermon.

Listen to her sermon: "Had Zimri peace, who slew his master?" Jezebel is reminding Jehu that Zimri had sinned and had paid the penalty. "We reap," she is saying, "according to our sowing. Our sin finds us out." Jezebel believed that was true in everybody's case except her own. Jehu even believed it was true of Jezebel herself. "Be sure your sin will find you out," said Jezebel. "Right," said Jehu. Then, as if by way of illustration, he shouted to those with that ill-starred queen, "Throw her down." There was a struggle, a shriek, a dull thud upon the cobblestones, and the dogs had a banquet of human blood, just as they did when they lapped up the blood of murdered Naboth, Jezebel's victim.

Then there are those who seem to fancy that they can escape change. There are mothers who never wish their children to grow up. There are also those, both men and women, who fight in utter desperation to keep from growing old. But we pass from childhood to youth, from youth to middle life, from middle life to old age whether we wish it or not. The more we resist getting old, the heavier old age sits upon us. Some time ago I visited a great preacher for whom I had a profound admiration. He was then sixty-nine years of age. But this good man disappointed me greatly by turning to me with the desperation of a cornered animal and saying, "It is awful for a man who has lived his life in the thick of things, as I have, to get old and to get where he can't carry on any longer." I believe God has as much a plan for December as for January. Therefore, I propose to grow old without fear.

Finally, there are those who refuse to face up to suffering. They go blithely forward through peaceful years. Then, like a bolt from the blue, tragedy comes. Something trips them up, and they fall flat. But instead of getting up and starting again, they lie in self-pity and bewail their lot. They cry weakly, "Why should this happen to me?" Thus they become a burden to themselves, a burden to others, and a disappointment to God. Thus there are those who, though seeking to dodge the inevitable, end by flunking the whole course.

2. There is a second group made up of men and women who are far more sturdy than these. They are those who face life's requirements bravely, but who seek to carry on in their own strength. They leave God out. These also fall short.

Theirs is the failure of the courageous, while the other is the failure of the cowardly. But both end in disappointment to themselves and to their Lord. The poet pictures such a man in *"Invictus."* This song is sometimes sung in churches as if it were Christian. It is not Christian at all. It has a certain sturdy courage about it, but it is thoroughly pagan and humanistic.

"Out of the night that covers me,
　Black as the pit from pole to pole,
I thank whatever gods may be
　For my unconquerable soul.

"In the fell clutch of circumstance
　I have not winced nor cried aloud.
Under the bludgeonings of chance
　My head is bloody, but unbowed.

"Beyond this place of wrath and tears
　Looms but the horror of the shade,
And yet the menace of the years
　Finds and shall find me unafraid.

"It matters not how strait the gate,
　How charged with punishments the scroll,
I am the master of my fate:
　I am the captain of my soul."

It sounds very brave for one to claim that he is the master of his fate and the captain of his soul. But, according to his own confession, this captain has nothing of which to boast. His present is altogether forbidding. In fact, it is as "black as the pit from pole to pole." His future has not even a horizon where he can hope for a dawn—

> "Beyond this place of wrath and tears
>> Looms but the horror of the shade."

Surely we need a better captain than that!

3. Then, there is a third group that not only accept these requirements but use them and thus come to their best.

III

How, then, can we meet and master the requirements of the school of life?

1. We need a firm confidence in God. In other words, we need an unfaltering faith in him who has planned the course for this man-making school that we call human life. We need to believe that the Headmaster has at least these three characteristics.

First, speaking for myself, if I am to make the best of this course, I must believe that it is planned by One who is interested in me personally. It was my privilege as a youth to attend the famous Webb School at Bell Buckle, Tennessee. I owe to "Old Sawney," as his boys affectionately called the headmaster of this school, an unpayable debt. I had not been long at Bell Buckle before Old Sawney took time to take me alone for a personal conference. He talked to me about his hopes for me and about my own possibilities. He had the reputation of being rigid in his discipline, as he was. But I was braced and heartened to face it by the assurance that he was interested in me personally. There were times when I had to lean my shoulders hard against this conviction.

This same bracing conviction is needed in the school of life. There are times when the course does seem exceedingly hard. There are times, in fact, when life for many becomes so difficult that there is no seeing it through except through faith in a God who is our Father and who loves us with an everlasting love. There is an all but infinite difference, when life goes to pieces, between the man who believes in the love of God and the man who can find no better explanation of the grim tragedy than that given by Thomas Hardy as he closes his book *Tess of the D'Urbervilles*—"Thus, the President of the universe had finished his sport with Tess."

Second, if I am to pursue this course successfully, I need a solid conviction, not only of the love of God, but also of his wisdom. To refer again to my old teacher, I knew that in attending Webb School there were certain requirements. Old Sawney was strong for the study of Latin and Greek. Naturally, there were those among both parents and pupils who objected to majoring on such subjects. Once an objecting father said, "I do not care for the classics. I want my son to have a practical education. I want him to know how to milk a cow."

"Right," said Old Sawney. "So do I want my son to know how to milk a cow, but I want him to know how to do something else that a calf can't beat him doing."

So I took the prescribed course in the faith that my headmaster knew what he was about. Many today would say he was vastly wrong. However, even yet, I am not convinced that he was.

Now just as I needed confidence in the wisdom of my teacher, so do I need confidence also in the wisdom of God. I need to believe that God knows me perfectly, and that his plan for me is the wisest possible. I need to believe that, even in the seemingly harsh and cruel, he is both loving and wise. When the mother eagle comes to her brood, not to bring them food, but to tear their home into shreds and to toss them out over the cliffs, that looks cruel and senseless. But what is she after? She is teaching them to fulfill their destiny. They are made for the cloudland and the upper air. Even so, I must believe that through the hard experiences that come to me, God is seeking to teach me flight sunward and God-ward. In wisdom and love he is trying to bring me to my best.

Finally, if I am to make the best of this prescribed course, I must believe, not only in the love and wisdom of God, but in his fair play. What was the trouble with the man of one talent? He made up his mind that his master would not play fairly with him. He was proud of his one talent until he found one friend who had two and another who had five. Then he went home in dismay to bury his talent in the ground. What could he do in competition with those who were so much more richly endowed than himself? When he explained his conduct, he said, "I was afraid. I was afraid that my master would require as much of me with my small gifts as he did of my friends with their large." Some of us feel that way about God. But he does not grade us according to our achievements, but according to our faithfulness. Hence, all have an equal chance. Every man to whom he can say, "You have been faithful," receives highest honors.

2. Thus believing in God, we are to commit our lives to him. In faith we are to become laborers together with him. This is what an honor student did in the long ago. Having loved with a love that issued in obedience, he tells us with radiant face what he has learned in the school of life. "We know," he declares, "that all things work together for good to them that love God." The same knowledge is open to us. While confessing that sometimes the requirements seem

grim and hard, we are sure that if we face them in the fellowship of God every one of them will minister to our enrichment. Thus, we shall find that this world with all its tragedies is the best possible world for the growing of a soul.

IV

I'D LEARN TO REMEMBER

"You must remember all the experiences through which the Lord your God has led you."

DEUTERONOMY 8:2 (SMITH-GOODSPEED)

WHAT A MARVELOUS POWER IS MEMORY! IT IS ABSO-lutely independent of space and time. It is far fleeter than the fastest airship. It can bridge seas and continents as quickly as the light. Not only is it independent of space, but of time also. Here is a man eighty years of age. How vain for him to sing, "Backward, turn backward, O time in your flight!" Yet memory can bridge the wide chasm of the years. Instantly it can transport this man back to the land of childhood. Instantly he can be looking again into faces long dust and hearing voices long since still.

Not only is memory independent of time and space, but of death also. The brain passes. We use up one every seven years. But memory abides. When the rich man died, he left behind him most of the treasures to which he had clung with passionate devotion. He left his purple and fine linen. He left his palace. He left his wealth. He left his five brothers. But he took with him into that unseen country his memory. So it will be with us. We cannot live in the body always, but always we shall remember.

If we may believe our scientists, memory never lets go of anything. It holds fast to all that we put into its wide-open hands. Every thought that we think, every word that we speak, every deed that we do, all these memory holds fast, never letting a single one of them go. No wonder Themistocles exclaimed when one proposed to teach him to remember, "Teach me rather to forget." But that no man can do. Here the words of Omar Khayyám are tremendously true:

> "The Moving Finger writes; and, having writ
> Moves on: nor all thy Piety nor Wit
> Shall lure it back to cancel half a Line,
> Nor all thy Tears wash out a Word of it."

Those rescued from drowning have testified that in the instant that they were sinking, seemingly for the last time, they saw all their yesterdays pictured as upon a screen. Some theologians believe that the Books of Judgment that Revelation tells us are to be opened by and by are none other than the books of memory where are recorded our every deed whether good or evil.

Now this marvelous power is given to us by a loving God. If we use it aright, it will become to us an angel of mercy guarding us from going wrong, or leading us back into the right path when our foolish feet have strayed. Rightly used, it will be a bit of heaven in our lives in the here and now and will make any future heaven vastly richer. But if we misuse it, that which is intended to be an angel may become a very devil.

In a previous sermon I reminded you that some of our worst vices are only virtues gone wrong. The courageous man may become utterly reckless and thus throw away a precious life that might have been of service to others. Even so, the amazing power of memory that, rightly used, enriches all life may be used in such a fashion as to bring nothing but harm. "As he thinketh in his heart, so is he." That is the equivalent of saying, "As a man remembereth in his heart, so is he." For memory simply means the power to recall or the power to keep in mind. How we remember, then, is of great importance.

II

This being the case, it is not surprising that God, through this amazing Book and through objects set visibly before our eyes, calls us to remember again and again. The book of Deuteronomy, from which our text is taken, is supremely a book of remembrance. Over and over the author warns us against the peril of forgetting. Over and over he calls us to remember. "You must remember all the experiences through which the Lord your God has led you." Not only does God call us to remember by word, but he puts keepsakes into our hands to assist us in remembering. For more than a thousand years before the coming of Jesus, the Jewish people had celebrated the Feast of the Passover. This feast was to help them to remember: "Thou shalt remember that thou wast a bondman in the land of Egypt and that the Lord, thy God, redeemed thee." When Jesus celebrated this supper for the last time, he pushed the paschal lamb out of its place and substituted himself. "This is my body," he declared, "My all, my very self, given for you. Do this in remembrance of me."

The most solemn service of the Church is to help us to remember.

But why, if we never forget anything, do we need this urgent call to remembrance? We need it because, while scientifically we never forget, practically we forget everything. There is nothing too big or too little for us to forget. We forget our engagements. We sometimes forget our bills. We forget our church vows and our marriage vows. We forget our lessons. We forget our friends. We even forget God.

Now the fact that we forget does not mean that the forgotten creature or event has been erased from the tablets of memory. The difference between a good memory and a poor memory is this—a good memory is able, figuratively speaking, to lay its hand upon the desired treasure while a poor memory cannot. We know how to sympathize with the youth who had just read in his physics the definition of space. "Define space," said the teacher. The student, having just read this definition, knew that he ought to remember it. But somehow he could not. Therefore, he answered, "I have it in my head, but I can't tell it."

But while the fact that we cannot recall the desired something does not mean that it has been erased, it does mean that it has ceased to be of any practical value for us. As a boy I went one day into the "racket store" to buy a pair of shoes. The lovable and slipshod merchant who owned the store showed me a shoe that suited me exactly. "All right," I said, "I will take the pair." Then he began a frantic search for the mate of that shoe. But he never could find it. I have no doubt it was there, but he had forgotten where it was. So he missed the sale.

Some time ago, while driving on a lonely stretch of road,

I had a puncture. I had an extra tire, but it was locked up and I had forgotten where I had put the key. So I set out to the nearest village to get help. I found a garageman and we came back together. When he had fixed the puncture and I reached in my pocket for the money with which to pay him, I found my key. I had had it all the time. But in spite of that, it was of no more help to me in this emergency than if I had lost it altogether. To forget, therefore, is to lose. To forget God is to act as if God did not exist. No wonder wise John Bunyan said that Forgetful Green is about the most dangerous spot on the road from the City of Destruction to Mount Zion.

Then we are urged to remember because what we remember is really a matter of choice. When, therefore, we think on God and the experiences through which he has led us, it is because we choose so to think. When we forget, it is because we make forgetfulness our choice. Sometimes we make this choice consciously—sometimes unconsciously. Some forget God because they are preoccupied. They crowd out the best with the worst or with the second best. It was thus that the man with the muckrake missed the angel that was poised above him, waiting to crown him. He was so intent upon his sticks and straw that he forgot the eternal and abiding.

Then there are times that we forget God by sheer force of will. That was the case with the fool of whom the psalmist wrote: "The fool hath said in his heart, There is no God." It is evident that the thought of God annoyed this ancient fool. If there was a God and he himself was his child, then he ought to live not as a son of mud but as a son of God. This made demands upon him that he did not wish to meet. Therefore, he dismissed God. He refused to think about him;

and God, for him, ceased to exist. He doomed himself by a wrong use of his memory.

III

Now, if we obey the sane words of our text and remember God and the experiences through which he has led us, what are some of the treasures that such remembering will put into our hands?

1. Gratitude. It is by remembering that we become grateful. Gratitude is not a trifling something that we can take up or lay down without being either the richer or the poorer. Gratitude is that which puts a song in the soul. To be thankless is to be joyless. It is also a mark of spiritual maturity. Naturally, we do not expect gratitude of little babies. We do not expect it of moral and spiritual dwarfs. But we do expect it of those who grow up. To have no gratitude is always to remain a spiritual infant.

One day a wise psalmist looking over the garden of his soul missed one flower that he knew he could not do without. If he did not miss this flower altogether, at least it was not growing in as rich profusion as he desired. Therefore, he decided to do something about it. He fairly laid violent hands upon his sluggish soul and woke it to the task and privilege of gratitude. "Bless the Lord, O my soul, and forget not all his benefits." Understand, he was not calling on his soul to remember all the benefits that God had bestowed. But he was asking that not all of these be forgotten. He was to remember at least some of them. He knew that in thinking upon God's mercies, thanksgiving would naturally follow. Right thinking always issues in real thanking.

Then remembering God's mercies makes for gratitude for

another reason. One of the greatest foes of gratitude is conceit. The rich farmer had no gratitude toward either God or man because he was so profoundly conceited. He forgot that it was God who had given him power to get wealth. He had forgotten that it was God who had sent the sunshine and the rain in just the right proportions. He had forgotten the loyalty of those men who had worked with him. He was a self-made man. Therefore, in his thoughtlessness, he had nobody to thank but himself. But if he had only remembered, his conceit would have given place to humility. In the realization that everything had come to him not through his own merit but as a gift, he would have been enriched by gratitude.

2. The memory of God's dealings with us will save us from fretfulness and feverishness and worry. It will minister to our courage and confidence. One day when Jesus was crossing the Sea of Galilee with his friends, he said, "Beware ye of the leaven of the Pharisees." The word "leaven" suggested bread. These friends realized that they had forgotten to lay in a sufficient supply of bread before setting out on their journey. Therefore, they were in a veritable fever of worry. It was then that Jesus turned to them with pained amazement and asked, "Do you not remember? You were quite short of bread out on the lakeside that day. Yet the five thousand were fed. You were equally destitute on another occasion when provisions were found for four thousand." But because they had forgotten, they were afraid.

Does the present moment find you in a hard situation? Is some deadly fear stalking your steps? Does disaster seem to be knocking at your door? Have your skies grown grim and gray? Then take a turn through your yesterdays. This is not the first time that you have been in a trying situation.

There was a time when you seemed to be in the very valley of the shadow. Yet God led you through. He is the same God still.

Are you afraid for our torn and bleeding world? Does the future look black for your nation? Indeed it does, but this is not the only dark day that has ever broken upon the world or upon our nation. We have been in trying situations before. The God who saw his people through yesterday will see them through tomorrow. Does the Church seem defeated and all but dead? There is nothing new about that. There was a time when the only real Christian in the world was hanging on a cross—yet God won through to victory.

3. As we remember God's gracious dealings with us, we are brought to repentance. Our Lord, speaking through his prophet to the cold church at Ephesus, reminded its members that they had left their first love. Then he made his tender appeal, "Remember, therefore, whence thou are fallen and repent. Remember when God was as real to you as any earthly friend." It might be good for some of us thus to remember. We need to remember that day when the heavens opened above our bowed heads and the dove of God's peace came to home in our hearts. The fact that God was real to us once will make us eager to find him again.

When the Prodigal had gone into the far country, it was memory that helped to turn his wayward steps back to his father's house. "When he came to himself, he said, How many hired servants of my father's have bread enough and to spare, and I perish with hunger!" His want made him think of his father's wealth. The ugliness and stench of the swine pen made him think of the loveliness of his old home whose open door was welcome and whose atmosphere was love. At last, as memory made him see dear distant faces and hear old loved voices, he could resist no longer, but rose and went to his father. Remembering God's mercies will lead us to repentance.

4. Finally, memory is a great preventive. That is a wise word that the Preacher utters, "Remember now thy Creator in the days of thy youth." "Remember" here is used not so much in the sense of recalling as of "bear in mind." It is a great blessing when some gracious memory takes us by the hand and leads us to the heights as the angel laid hold on the hands of lingering Lot. It is a marvelous triumph when memory leads the Prodigal away from the stench of the swine pen to his father's house. But while that is good, it is only a second best. The best use of memory is that which keeps us out of the far country altogether. It is good to see the Prodigal come home, but I have an idea that he met many a fine chap on his way down that he did not see when he turned again home.

In one of his books Hugo gives a vivid description of a cannon loose at sea. The head gunner had forgotten to make this ten-thousand-pound monster secure. Therefore, when the ship began to be tossed by the sea, the gun broke loose from its moorings. Being on wheels, it began to plunge in such fashion as to threaten the very life of the vessel. Five men, one after another, had tried to bring it under control only to be crushed to death. Then while the sailors looked on with tense, white faces, the head gunner, through whose forgetfulness the tragedy had taken place, went down on the gun deck to fight with the monster.

There they stood facing each other—monster and man. The cannon seemed to be alive. "It had the agility of a mouse, the weight of an elephant, the ferocity of a tiger." The gunner could not kill it—it was already dead. In its fury it was grinding to pieces the bodies of the men it had already slain. Then the gunner got his crowbar between the spokes, turned the cannon on its side, and the fight was won. "What shall we do with this brave gunner?" asked the officer of the general in command. "Decorate him for his courage," he replied, "then have him shot for his carelessness."

This gunner remembered, but he remembered too late to save the lives of five men who might have been saved if he had remembered from the beginning. There is a story of a mother who one day took her son to the art gallery to see Holman Hunt's picture "The Light of the World." This mother explained the picture to the lad. She explained how all that Jesus could do in the presence of that shut door was to stand and knock. There was no knob on the outside. If the door was ever opened, it must be opened from within. Then she concluded, "Son, when Jesus, the Light of the World, comes to knock at your door, you must open it." Then the lad looked at his mother with glad confidence in his eyes and answered, "Yes, but I have never shut the door in his face." That is the highest use of memory. But if youth has passed and you have made many a blunder, then I say to you, as I say to my own heart, "Remember now." If we remember now, God can still do for us exceeding abundantly above all that we can ask or think.

V

I'D LIVE TODAY

*"This is the day that the Lord has made;
Let us rejoice and be glad therein!"*

PSALM 118:24 (SMITH-GOODSPEED)

HERE IS A MAN WITH A WORD OF WISDOM, NOT ONLY FOR every youth, but for those of us who are older grown. Though he lived in a long-gone past, he had a philosophy of life that is just as fresh and up to date today as it was twenty-five centuries ago. In fact, I am persuaded that his philosophy is even more needed in our crowded and hectic day than it was in the more quiet time in which he was privileged to live. Let us look at him as he awakens with his face radiant, not only with the outward light of the dawning of a new day, but radiant also from the inward light of joy that this new day has brought. "This," he cries with glad enthusiasm as he seems to take God's priceless gift in his hands, "this is the day that the Lord has made; let us rejoice and be glad therein!"

If I were young—in fact, whatever my age—I should certainly try to learn this man's secret. What is that secret?

He has learned to live a day at a time. Listen to his wise words. He does not say, "That was the day that the Lord had made." It is easy for us to believe that God made some grand days in a far-off yesterday. But this man is not tormented by a backward look. No more did he say, "That will be the day that the Lord will make." He rather lives and laughs in the here and now. "This," he says, "is the day that the Lord has made; let us rejoice and be glad therein!" Regardless of what yesterday may have been or of what tomorrow may be, he is going to live joyfully in today. He has learned to live one day at a time.

That, I take it, is a lesson well worth learning. I do not believe that it is wise, generally speaking, to buy on the installment plan. Such a system often leads to a burdensome debt and beyond that to extravagance. Thackeray said very wisely, "Nobody spends money quite so freely as one who is hopelessly and comfortably in debt." Personally, I have made a habit across the years of paying cash. Where I could not pay cash, I was, generally speaking, wise enough to do without. But while I do not believe in buying on the installment plan, there are many other matters connected with living where this plan must be employed.

For instance, when I came to church today, the distance was not great. Yet it was too great for me to jump it at a single bound. I had to come one step at a time. Some time ago I was driving over a mountainous road that would bend now to the right and now to the left. There were literally scores of curves. I should like to have finished with those troublesome curves all at once. But this was impossible. It was utterly impossible for me to take even two of those curves at once.

When as a youth I went to Webb School, my knowledge of Latin was just about naked nothing. In spite of this fact I entered a class that was reading Caesar. I was ashamed to enter the beginner's class—the boys in that class looked so much younger than I! Naturally, my first few weeks were a painful trudge through the valley of humiliation. In fact, I had been in the class for ten whole weeks before I answered one single question. But Old Sawney, the wise headmaster, took me alone one day for a private conference. "If you will learn one word a day," he encouraged, "you can hold the class." That seemed simple enough. I tried it with the result that before the end of my second year I was leading the class. Even so, it is the height of wisdom in the business of living to live one day at a time. This is true for at least three reasons.

I

It is wise to live a day at a time because one day is all I have. That is all you have. It is the sum total of the treasure of the richest as well as the poorest. So far as time is concerned, our sole possession is today.

This is the case because yesterday has gone. It is as completely beyond my reach as the first day of Year One. It is as completely beyond my reach as that distant day when the "morning stars sang together, and all the sons of God shouted for joy." I can no more recall yesterday than I can recall that first Christmas morning when the angel said to the shepherds, "Fear not: for, behold, I bring you good tidings of great joy." My past is beyond my recall just as is yours. There is no going back to it. This is true regardless of what my attitude to yesterday may be. It is true regardless of what your attitude may be.

Perhaps yesterday bored some of us. Perhaps we went through it with yawns, finding it as dull and oppressive as a dust storm. Worse still, we may have found it not only tiresome but painful. Maybe it brought us some bitter disappointments. Maybe it introduced us to stark tragedy. This being the case, now that it is in the past we are glad. We sigh with relief that we do not have to live one of its oppressive or painful hours again.

Then there are others who look back to yesterday with wistful eyes. Their past is full of delightful memories. There were days that were radiant with joy. Even those that were commonplace look beautiful now, for they have taken on the enchantment that distance lends. It is so easy for us to idealize yesterday! This is especially true of those of us who are growing old. We talk tenderly of the good old days. Jerome K. Jerome says that men have been looking back to the good old days of fifty years ago ever since Adam's fifty-first birthday. Of course, these good old days were not so good when we were actually living them! It was the days of our fathers that were good then. But now that they have once been ours and are ours no more, we look back to them through wistful eyes.

Then there are those who look upon yesterday with longing eyes because they realize that they did not use it well. Some are conscious of the fact that they spent its treasure for a poor second best while others must confess that they failed to "fill the unforgiving minute with sixty seconds' worth of distance run." Worse still, there are those who not only refused to use yesterday well but chose to use it to rob and wound others as well as themselves. Naturally these would like to get back into yesterday to tidy up a bit. They would like to give a few flowers that they failed to give. They would like to rub out a few ugly stains and to heal a few wounds. They would like another try at the game that they realize they played but poorly.

But, regardless of what our attitude toward yesterday may be, it has gone from us forever. We may dismiss it with a sigh of relief as we say with Jacob, "Few and evil have the days of the years of my life been." Again we may grasp at it frantically as did that good-natured sensualist Esau. You recall his story: "When he would have inherited the blessing, he was rejected; for he found no place for repentance though he sought it carefully with tears." This does not mean that he found no forgiveness, but that he found no way of getting into yesterday to change it. Though he pounded at the door of the past with bruised fist and tampered at its lock with bleeding thumb and finger, it remained fast closed.

Not only is yesterday beyond our reach because it has gone, but tomorrow is equally so because it has not arrived. Generally speaking, it is the older of us who tend to look back to yesterday. It is the young who are most absorbed in tomorrow. Perhaps some of you are now in high school, but you are not thrilled over that. Instead you are bored. Therefore, you are not studying now. Why should you? There will be plenty of time for that when you get into college. Some of you who are in college are going to wait until you get in the graduate school. You are going to be in dead earnest when you begin to specialize in law, medicine, theology, and what not. Then, there are those who have reached this stage who are still trifling. But this is only for today.

Tomorrow, when they get into the actual business of doing their life's work, they are going to be all enthusiasm. Thus do we, by postponing life, tend to squander our finest opportunities and to miss the choicest joys. None of us can live tomorrow; it has not come.

What is ours? Answer, *Today*. This wise psalmist realized this; he refused to try to recover yesterday. With the same wisdom he refused to try to live in some tomorrow that had not and would never come. He took what was actually his— and that was today. That is all I have. That is all you have. If you and I were on a rubber raft in the sea and had just one loaf of bread and one gallon of water, we should doubtless ration it so as to use it in the wisest possible way. Here we are on the wide sea of eternity. What are our resources so far as time is concerned? They are today. We ought, therefore, to live today because that is all we have.

II

We ought to live today, not only because today is all we have, but because it is all we can manage.

Suppose we had it in our power to get back our yesterdays. Suppose we were able to project ourselves into tomorrow. Suppose we could get all the days of our past and our future into our hands at once. What a boon that would be! No, it would not. It would not be a blessing but a curse. The other day I watched a juggler keep about a dozen balls in the air at once. That required skill. But no amount of skill can enable us to handle a dozen days at once. The truth is we can manage but one day at a time.

This is a lesson that it takes some of us a whole lifetime to learn. Therefore, instead of centering our entire attention

59

upon living one day at a time, we try to manage at least two days. Some of us seek to manage yesterday and today at the same time. But we never make a success of it. Years ago I watched one of the brightest men I have ever known go stark mad in a vain effort to live yesterday and today at the same time. His yesterday had tragedy in it. He confessed to a friend through lips white and drawn with pain, "There is something in my past I must forget." But somehow he could not let yesterday go. Thus, failing to forget, he became a madman.

The results are equally tragic if we try to live today and tomorrow. That was what Jesus was warning against when he said, "Do not worry about tomorrow. . . . Let each day be content with its own ills." Some time ago I was called to conduct a funeral for one who had died by his own hand. As I looked into that pathetic face, I said in my heart, "What did you do that for?" I knew something of the answer. Had those dumb lips spoken, they would probably have said, "I was having a hard time today. But worse still, I saw a troop of tomorrows coming to me even more drab and gray and forbidding than today. The present and the future taken together were more than I could stand. Therefore, I flung out of life altogether!" How many thousands crack up every year because they try to manage two days at once—sometimes even three! They try to live yesterday, today, and tomorrow all at the same time. No wonder they find the task too great!

This wise psalmist avoided that nerve-racking and soul-destroying blunder. This he did by concentrating on today. Nobody is brawny enough to live three days at a time or even two. But any of us, by the help of God, can live one day.

The biggest liar in town can tell the truth for one day. The most dishonest of men can keep his hands out of the pocket of the other fellow for one day. The most self-centered and unkind can be kind for one day. The most prayerless can live prayerfully for one day. The most bitterly disappointed and sorely wounded can, by God's grace, endure his heartache for one day. Therefore, let us in glad confidence join our voices with that of the psalmist as he sings,

> "This is the day that the Lord has made;
> Let us rejoice and be glad therein!"

Not only are we to live today because today is all we have and because it is all we can manage, but we are to live today because it is all we need. We often bewail the brevity of life. "Man that is born of a woman is of few days." That is true. But it is not the quantity of life but its quality that really counts.

> "We live in deeds, not years; in thoughts, not breaths;
> In feelings, not in figures on a dial."

One man can live more in an hour than another in a century. All we need for the enjoyment of life eternal is a day.

This is the case because God's richest promises are not for yesterday nor for tomorrow but for today. When is it that he offers to you and to every man salvation? When is it that he makes eternal life available for you and me and all men? It is neither in the past nor in the future. It is in the here and now. "Did you know," I asked an earnest soul one day, "that God had set a particular date for your salvation?"

"No," came the answer.

"Well, he has. If I show you what that date is," I continued, "will you keep the engagement?"

When an affirmative answer was given, this was my reply, "Here is the date that God has set. 'Now is the accepted time; behold, now is the day of salvation.'" Today is all we need in order to come into possession of eternal life.

Then, today is all we need because, if we claim the presence of our Lord today, we thereby take care of yesterday. We can leave the past with God. That is what Paul meant when he said, "Forgetting those things which are behind." That is what Jesus meant when he said to the woman taken in the very act of shame, "Neither do I condemn thee; go, and sin no more." When God forgives, he forgets. "I will forgive their iniquity, and I will remember their sin no more." What God forgets, he gives us the privilege of forgetting.

On the night of his betrayal Jesus took with him into the inner precincts of the garden his three most intimate friends —Peter, James, and John. He was fighting a lonely fight and he longed for their companionship. But while he prayed, these friends went to sleep. "What," he said to Simon with a touch of heartache in his voice, "could ye not watch with me one hour?" But when he had left them, they went to sleep again. Then came the mob. Then also came Jesus, saying, "Sleep on now, and take your rest: . . . the Son of man is betrayed into the hands of sinners." By this he seemed to say, "Sleep on. You have missed your chance. You won't have missed it any more completely if you sleep forever." But in the very next breath he said, "Rise let us be going." If we dare live with God today, he takes care of yesterday.

Then just as God takes care of yesterday, so will he take care of tomorrow. To urge upon you to live a day at a time may seem to some to take a too short view of life. What was the matter with Esau, to whom we referred a few moments ago? The usual answer is that he lived only for today and forgot his tomorrow. He refused to look ahead. But that does not tell the whole story. It is true that he forgot tomorrow, but his real tragedy was that he misused today. Had he used his today rightly, his tomorrow would have taken care of itself. But squandering today, he lost tomorrow.

Listen to this brave sentence: "By faith Moses, when he was come to years, refused to be called the son of Pharaoh's daughter; choosing rather to suffer affliction with the people of God, than to enjoy the pleasures of sin for a season; esteeming the reproach of Christ greater riches than the treasures in Egypt: for he had respect unto the recompence of the reward." Literally translated—"He looked away from everything else to the coming reward." Thus it would seem that Moses was saved by looking ahead. But such was not in reality the case. It was not the looking ahead that gave him his great destiny; it was the making of a right choice in the present. Acting in today, he guaranteed his tomorrow.

Here, then, is a roadway to effective living. All we are called upon to do is in the fellowship of God to live today. This is the case because today is all we have. Today is all we can manage. Today is all we need. How this simplifies our task! How it conserves our energies by enabling us to say, "This one thing I do!" If we live rightly today, yesterday and tomorrow we can leave in God's hands. But if we refuse to use today, no obedience of yesterday, no dedication for tomorrow is of any value. Here is our one chance— "a little gleam of light between two eternities and no second chance forevermore."

"This is the day that the Lord has made;
Let us rejoice and be glad therein!"

Then this word as to technique! How can we learn to live a day at a time? Humbly I offer the following suggestions. Begin each day with a look into God's Word. Let him speak to you as you speak to ·him. Put yourself anew into his hands. Go over the plans for the day in his presence, seeking his guidance. Then through the day bear in mind that he is with you. "Speak to him, thou, for he heareth." When the day is done, leave it with its victories and defeats, its follies and sins, in his hands. Do not take any of its cares to bed with you. Finally, refuse to be discouraged. Be patient with yourself and also with God.

"Build a little fence of trust
    Around to-day;
Fill the space with loving work,
    And therein stay;

Look not through the sheltering bars
    Upon to-morrow;
God will help thee bear what comes
    Of joy or sorrow."

VI

I'D ENCOURAGE MYSELF

"But David encouraged himself in the Lord his God."

I SAMUEL 30:6

I

OF ALL THE BENEFACTORS THAT WE MEET ALONG THE road, few are more helpful than the courage bringer. Blessed is the man that is able to put heart into the despairing! Blessed is he who can dry our tears without resorting to the awkward expedient of a pocket handkerchief! One of the choicest souls in the New Testament is Barnabas. So proficient was he in bringing courage to the discouraged and defeated that those who knew him best gave him a new name. It is one of rare beauty. They called him a name that means "son of encouragement." He was incarnate consolation. To shake hands with him was to become possessed of a new courage. Even to meet him on the street was as refreshing as water to the thirsty or food to the hungry. To tarry for a brief hour in his presence was to go away with a new sparkle in the eye and a new elasticity in the step.

65

The courage bringer is a benefactor because courage is essential to the business of living. It is more than a luxury; it is a necessity. When we lose courage, we lose our joy and our zest. When we lose courage and become short on hope, the feast of life loses its tang. If our courage gives way altogether, we are likely to fling out of life from sheer wretchedness. I had a brilliant young physician in my church some years ago who died by his own hand. He dared to quit before the whistle blew. What was the cause? He was afflicted with a disease that he considered incurable. Thus afflicted, he did not have the courage to travel the long road of torture with nothing but death in prospect at the end of his struggle. Courage is, therefore, essential to zestful living. Without a measure of it, some refuse to live at all.

Then, courage is essential to our usefulness. However gifted we may be, if we have lost our courage, if we have made up our minds that the Kingdom of God will never come, if we have decided that the crooked can never be made straight, then our days of usefulness are over. Elijah was a mighty man. He towered above the men of his generation as a majestic mountain towers above an anthill. But one day he fell under the juniper tree with hope and courage all gone out of him. "I have had enough," he told the Lord frankly. "Take away my life. I am no better than my fathers. They suffered Israel to go into idolatry. I have not been able to bring it back." So what? God could not use this mighty man for any further service till he had enabled him to recover his courage.

Not only do we lose our usefulness when we lose our courage, but we become positive liabilities. Courage is contagious, but so is cowardice. When I was a young teacher, the new readers were just beginning to react against the stories of McGuffey. While McGuffey delighted in stories with a moral, the writers of these new readers seemed to delight in stories that were nonmoral or sometimes merely silly. One of these did have a moral of a certain type, though I am not sure that such was intended. But I remember the story to this day—largely, I think, because of its excruciating childishness. It ran something like this:

Chicken Little was out in the garden one day when a cabbage leaf fell on her tail. This world-shaking event filled her with utter terror. Therefore, she began to run with all her might. By and by as she ran she met Hen Pen. This wise bird, seeing the despair in the face of Chicken Little, asked the cause. Having been informed that the sky was falling, Hen Pen joined in the stampede. Then they met Duck Luck, then Goose Loose, then Turkey Lurkey. At last they met Fox Lox. When they had informed him of the tragedy, he told them of the lovely air-raid shelter that he had prepared for just such an emergency. Therefore, they all ran into his den and the fox lived happily for many days thereafter. It is a story of unparalleled silliness, but there is this much truth about it—Let the most insignificant person stampede, and others have a great tendency to stampede also. Cowardice is very contagious.

If, however, you paid attention to my text, you will remind me that it does not say that David encouraged others. It only says that he encouraged himself. But this fact adds to the worth and gallantry of David's achievement rather than detracting from it. If we say blessed is the courage bringer, blessed even more is the man who can encourage himself. It is easy to see why this is the case. Sometimes others fail us. Sometimes others do not even know how desperately short on courage we are. Happy, therefore, is the man who learns the fine art of encouraging himself! Such a man is a self-starter.

I remember the first self-starting car I ever drove. I was living in a country town in Texas. A call came one day for a wedding some ten or twelve miles in the country. My own car was out of order. The garage man who was repairing it told me it was impossible to get it in condition in time to be used. Then he added, "I have a new car, a self-starter. You may use that." So I accepted his kind offer and set out on my journey! Now it so happened that on the way I had to cross a creek with a muddy bottom. In my haste to get through I killed the engine. At first I was filled with terror. It appalled me to think how my wedding finery would look after I had waded knee-deep in muddy water to crank the car. Then I remembered that it was a self-starter. What a thrill when I stepped on the starter and was once more on my way! David did not have to have somebody to come to the rescue. He encouraged himself.

Now by encouraging himself he not only helped himself, but he was able to bring courage to others as well. We cannot give to our fellows what we do not possess. It is useless for me to shout courage to you when my own knees are smiting together in terror. But if I have learned to be steady and unafraid, then I can share my courage with others. There is a familiar story that years ago a group of terrified people were huddled together one night in the cabin of a little sailing vessel as the life of that vessel was being threatened by a storm. By and by one of their number dared to crawl out on deck. A moment later he came back with a new light in his eye. "We are going to weather the tempest," he declared. "In the flare of the lightning, I caught a glimpse of the face of the pilot, and he smiled." The courage of the pilot was contagious. Even so it was with David. By encouraging himself, he was able to bring courage to others.

II

When did David encourage himself?

This is an important question. David was such a many-sided man, he was a man of such outstanding ability, his career was so brilliantly successful, that we are apt to say: "Of course he encouraged himself. If I possessed his vast gifts, if I were in his circumstances, if everything always came to me right side up as it did to him, then I could encourage myself as he did. But look at the mess that I am in. My life is all tangles and knots." This also David might have said about himself. Certainly in this instance he did not find courage because of his circumstances, but in spite of them. He had much to discourage him, as we can see if we look at his situation.

1. David had just made a terrible and depressing failure. He was at war. He had under his protection a certain city of great importance to himself and to his men. But through his own neglect or for some other reason he had not succeeded in protecting that city. One day he came back from a foray to find it in ruins. Perhaps not a house was left standing. Certainly all the inhabitants had been either killed or carried away into captivity to face a fate worse than death. Thus David knew the depressing experience of failure. A kindred experience comes to all of us sooner or later, bringing with

it an urgent call for courage. David, therefore, needed to encourage himself because he had failed.

2. David needed to encourage himself because of what his failure had cost him. The first price he had paid for failure was loss of popularity. David had a wonderful capacity for winning *the hearts* and confidence of people. Everything that he did pleased the people, the author tells us. That was the case because David pleased them personally. Approving him, they approved what he did. But now all this had changed. His popularity had now become antagonism. The hurrahs of his fellows had all changed to hisses. So antagonistic had these onetime friends and followers become that they were now threatening to stone him to death. He was in positive danger of his life.

A second price that David had paid for his failure was the loss both of his goods and of those whom he loved. His property had been in this city, even as that of his followers. His wives and children had also been there. But his property had been destroyed and his loved ones had been carried into captivity along with those of his soldiers. David was by no means sure that he would ever see those loved faces again. There was thus an emptiness for him where there had once been a home. It is said of his followers that they wept until they had no more tears to weep. We may believe that David's tears were just as plentiful as theirs.

3. Then David needed to encourage himself in order to keep from giving way to bitterness and angry resentment. These thoughtless soldiers were blaming their leader for a disaster that was just as painful to him as it was to them, perhaps far more so. They were acting as if he alone were responsible. They were acting as if they alone had suffered.

How easy it would have been for David to have turned on them in angry resentment and told them how cruelly unreasonable they were. But instead he encouraged himself.

Now since David managed to encourage himself when his circumstances were so bad, we also may have hope. In fact, whatever may be our circumstances, this door stands open to us. If the situation in which we find ourselves refuses to encourage us, if all human lips are dumb, if nobody utters a word of commendation, even if everybody utters the opposite, we still have this privilege—we may encourage ourselves.

III

How did David encourage himself?

We may be sure that he refused certain methods that we are sometimes prone to try. For instance, he did not encourage himself by getting his feelings hurt and washing his hands of the whole business. To that, I am sure, he was greatly tempted. It is a temptation that comes to all of us. I suppose there are few pastors who have not at times felt tempted to encourage themselves by saying, "If things do not go as they ought, then I am going to stand from under." There are few faithful workers in the church who have not at times felt this. It is a temptation, I dare say, that comes to almost every man who undertakes to put through a worth-while task. "Why should I carry on when nobody seems to care?" But David refused to encourage himself by threatening to quit.

No more did David encourage himself by shutting his eyes to the ugly facts that were making courage difficult. He might have told himself that after all he had not lost the fight, after all the city had not been really destroyed. He might have said, "In spite of all appearances to the contrary, these soldiers of mine are not hot and angry and ready to stage a rebellion." But he was too stern a son of fact to encourage himself by trying to slip into a fool's paradise. He did not tell himself that everything was right when he knew that almost everything was wrong. To shut our eyes to facts simply because they are ugly is not courageous but cowardly and foolish.

Here is a heartening characteristic of Jesus—he never glossed over unpleasant facts. As eager as he was for followers, he was never so eager that he allowed any one to become his disciple without knowing the price to be paid. When a young chap came, all enthusiasm, and said, "Lord, I will follow thee whithersoever thou goest," our Lord chilled that enthusiasm by saying, "Foxes have holes, and birds of the air have nests; but the Son of man hath not where to lay his head." In other words, "I may have to go supperless to bed tonight. My bed may not be in a comfortable home but on the mountainside. Are you ready to follow under those conditions?" And at that the young fellow went away.

As he never disguised the hard conditions of discipleship, no more did he disguise the fact of the world's grim need. "The Son of man is come," he said, "to seek and to save that which was lost." He understood the tragedy of the quarrel between man and God and also between man and man. Jesus was a stern son of fact. We love, therefore, to see David sharing this candor with him. He would not bolster his courage by telling himself what he knew to be a lie. How, then, did David encourage himself?

1. I have an idea that, having faced his losses, having faced his defeat, having looked over his liabilities, he did not spend all his time looking at these. He next began to take stock of what he had left. Having missed one train, he did not give up the journey. He looked about to see what other conveyance was possible. If we are going to encourage ourselves, we must not look simply at our losses and our failures, but also at the possibilities that are still ours.

2. David told himself that, though he had made one failure, that failure need not be final. He believed in the possibility of a new start. He was confident that there was a wonderful place called the Land of Beginning Again. He had some of the fine courage of that woman in the New Testament who, in quest of health, had made one failure after another for twelve long years yet had refused to give up. When one day she heard of Jesus, she took courage. A natural thing for her to have said was, "There is no use trying any more. I have consulted one physician after another for long years and they have relieved me of nothing but my money. I am through." But she encouraged herself by saying, "If I can just touch his cloak, I will get well." Thus, refusing to count any number of failures as final, she won.

3. Finally, and biggest and best of all, David brought his desperate plight into the presence of God. "David encouraged himself in the Lord his God." That is a source of encouragement that is always open to all of us. It is a source that never fails. It is said that the personal presence of Julius Caesar could change the most commonplace soldier into a hero. Whether this was the case or not, I do not know. But of this I am perfectly sure—that a realization of the

personal presence of God can make the most timid of us courageous. "I have set the Lord always before me; because he is at my right hand, I shall not be moved."

Here is a great scene. An ancient merchant vessel in the Mediterranean Sea is being pounded to pieces by a hurricane. This tempestuous demon has been tearing at the weakened vessel now for fourteen days and nights. The nerves of the men on board, both sailors and passengers, are now shot to pieces. For days these have been too sick and too fear-filled to take proper nourishment. Though brave men by nature, under these trying circumstances their courage has been shattered. "All hope," said Luke, who was on board that wrecking vessel, "all hope that we should be saved was then taken away." Thus we see them there huddled together in despair, waiting for the tragic death that I am sure many of them hoped would soon come.

Then something happens. A queer chap comes up out of the hole of the vessel, where he has been engaged in prayer. He makes his way along the slippery deck, grips a broken spar, then lifts his voice above the crash of the thunder and the shriek of the wind, and shouts this great word: "Be of good cheer; for there shall be no loss of any man's life among you, but of the ship. For there stood by me this night the angel of God, whose I am, and whom I serve, saying, Fear not, Paul; thou must be brought before Caesar; and, lo, God hath given thee all them that sail with thee. Wherefore, sirs, be of good cheer: for I believe God, that it shall be even as it was told me." Here is a man who when all human help and hope were gone encouraged himself in the Lord his God. By thus encouraging himself, Paul also encouraged others. By thus encouraging others, he saved the day. The story has this happy ending: "They all escaped safe to land."

One of the psalmists tells us of a man who in a time of upheaval somehow kept his courage. When others were cracking up and going to pieces, he looked upon the whole tragic scene with steady heart and quiet eyes. When his fellows saw this man so courageous, they naturally asked for his secret. He gave it in these words: "The Lord of hosts is with us; the God of Jacob is our refuge." "Therefore," he added with a kind of holy swagger, "I am not going to fear though the earth be removed and the mountains be carried into the midst of the sea."

This man had learned David's secret. He knew how to encourage himself in the Lord his God. We, too, may learn it. The door to this high achievement stands open before your face and mine. We ought to hasten to enter that door because we are so greatly in need of courage. We ought to enter it also because no other source of courage is so sure and so satisfying. We ought to enter it because by so doing we can enrich both ourselves and our fellows. Blessed, therefore, is the man of whom it may be said, "He encouraged himself in the Lord his God."

VII

I'D FACE UP TO LIFE

"As a good soldier of Christ Jesus accept your share of suffering."

II TIMOTHY 2:3 (WEYMOUTH)

I

THIS IS A PART OF PAUL'S STIRRING APPEAL TO TIMOTHY. Timothy was the product of a divided home. His father and mother were of different nationalities and different religions. That is generally a heavy handicap for the husband and wife, and still more so for the children. It is a part of the divine plan that the married couple is to be one. They are to be one in their mutual selfgiving. They are to be one in their devotion to God. For one to be religious and the other not, or for each to be possessed of a different religious faith, is often fruitful in tragedy.

We are happy to report, however, that the fact that Timothy's father was a pagan did not result in disaster for his gifted son. This was due, it would seem, not to any help from the father, but to the devotion of Timothy's mother and grandmother. I think that the very fact that these two knew that the father was a religious liability rather than an asset intensified their earnestness. They knew that if they saved this gifted child for the faith, they must take it upon themselves. Therefore, they gave themselves to the task of carefully training Timothy for a religious life. "From a child," Paul writes, "thou hast known the holy scriptures, which are able to make thee wise unto salvation through faith which is in Christ Jesus." Blessed is the mother who claims her child for God in his young and tender years! And blessed is the child of such a mother! He has an advantage that the child who is robbed of such a privilege can never know.

But in spite of the careful training that Timothy received from his mother Eunice and his grandmother Lois, they did not succeed in winning Timothy to a definite committal to Christ. They prepared the way of the Lord. They sowed the seed that was to issue in a rich harvest. But it was Paul who had the joy of introducing this gifted youth to Jesus Christ. It was Paul who became his father in the faith. Paul was privileged to win many converts; but none, I think, had such a warm place in his roomy heart as did Timothy.

How Paul and Timothy first met we are not told. The meeting took place at Lystra during Paul's first missionary journey. Sholem Asch imagines that it was youthful Timothy who ministered to Paul after he was stoned. When his enemies had left Paul for dead, when they thought they had seen the last of him, there was one who stood by in the hope that he might help. By and by when consciousness came back to Paul, there was a hand that was touching his bruised and bleeding face as tenderly as the hand of a mother. That was the hand of Timothy. It seems to have been a case of love at first sight between the two. But it was a love that grew richer and deeper through the years.

Later when Paul returned to Lystra on his second missionary journey, he found that young Timothy had already won a place for himself in the local church. He had gained the good opinion of all the saints. He was a promising candidate for the ministry. Therefore, Paul took him and ordained him to this high calling. From then on until Paul laid down his life in Rome, Timothy was his constant helper, often his most intimate associate. When Paul, therefore, wrote, "As a good soldier of Christ Jesus, accept your share of suffering," he was writing to a young Christian minister who had been converted under his own influence and who had been ordained to the ministry by his own hands.

II

"As a good soldier of Christ Jesus, accept your share of suffering." What is Paul saying to this young man?

1. He is telling him that to be a Christian is to be a soldier of Jesus Christ. That is, Timothy from henceforth is not to belong to himself but to Another. Timothy is not to do his own will but the will of Another. The moment one becomes a soldier, he knows he can no longer do as he pleases. He must live under orders. His own will ceases to be the law of his life. So Paul tells Timothy that in becoming a Christian he has given his life to Jesus Christ.

2. Since becoming a Christian means being a soldier, it means that we are to live in a soldierly fashion. When one joins the army, he is not expecting an easy time. He faces the certainty of hard training, of long marches. He faces

the possibility of hard battles, of bloody wounds, of death. Such, says Paul, must be the case with the Christian soldier. To be a Christian is not the easiest way through life. To be a Christian means conflict.

That is what we sometimes forget. Often the minister, in his eagerness to win disciples, unconsciously pictures the Christian life as one that is easy. But Jesus never made that mistake. He yearned for disciples with infinite intensity. Yet one day when a young man came, all enthusiasm, saying, "Lord, I will follow thee whithersoever thou goest," Jesus knew that he had not faced all the facts. He knew that he was expecting an easy adventure. Therefore, he said in substance, "I am more homeless than the foxes, I am more destitute than the birds of the air. If you follow me, you will have to endure hardship." At that the young man slunk away and we hear from him no more.

On another occasion when one asked Jesus, "Are there few that be saved?" he did not give a yes or no answer. Instead he said, "Strive to enter in at the strait gate." Strive —that is a strenuous word! It is a word with muscles astrut and with face flecked with sweat and blood. It means to strive as an athlete struggles on the athletic field. It means to fight as a soldier fights on the field of battle. "Strive to enter in at the strait gate for many . . . will seek to enter in and shall not be able."

This is the case for the very simple reason that the gate is narrow. "Narrow is the way," said Jesus. This is not the case because God has arbitrarily made it so. It is true in the nature of things. If you want to learn the multiplication table, narrow is the way. If you want to putt a golf ball successfully, narrow is the way. As a boy I made up my mind in a halfhearted fashion that I would learn to play the violin. I soon quit. This I did, not because I lost all desire to be a violinist, but because I discovered that narrow is the way.

3. Finally, Paul urges Timothy to accept his share of the suffering because he knows that it was up to Timothy whether he does this or not. You do not have to face up to life. You do not have to take your share of the hardship. Many flatly refuse. We may take an easier and less heroic way. There are multitudes whose supreme ambition seems to be to get through life with the least possible difficulty. Their ambition is to find a residence on Easy Street. But the trouble with Easy Street is that it has a way so often of ending on Rotten Row. To make ease the test of our conduct and thus to refuse to face up to life is to lose ourselves. But to take the opposite course is, as Paul tells Timothy, both to save ourselves and those that hear us.

III

"As a good soldier of Christ Jesus, accept your share of suffering." Why did Paul write this urgent word to Timothy?

1. He did it for the very simple reason that he and all of us are at times tempted to shirk. We are all, even the bravest, tempted to take the easy way. I know there is that within us to which the heroic appeals. Carlyle was right when he said: "It is not to taste sweet things but to do true and noble things and to vindicate ourselves under God's heaven as God-made men and women is that after which every son of Adam dimly longs." But along with this to which the heroic appeals there is that also which makes us shrink from taking our

share of hardship. Many are willing for others to be over-loaded, for others to do more than their part while they themselves do nothing at all.

2. But there is more in this than the natural tendency to shirk that belongs to us all. Timothy had certain handicaps that exposed him in a peculiar way to this temptation. Paul, who knew him well and loved him well, realized this fact. Timothy had three decided handicaps that made it hard for him to face up to life.

First, Timothy was timid. It would seem that he was easily frightened by the crowd. He found it as hard at times to face a congregation as some would to face a firing squad. There are those who make light of timidity. This is especially true of those who have never known its tortures. Personally, I know a little how to sympathize with Timothy. I have been gripped by utter terror at the very thought of appearing in public. I have had my knees shake so on such an occasion that I have seen some in the audience nudge each other and call attention to my trembling. Timothy would have known how to sympathize.

One day when Paul had sent him on a mission to that rather difficult church at Corinth, his heart fairly bled for him. He knew how harsh and unsympathetic some of the officials of that church could be. Therefore, he hastened to dispatch a letter containing this urgent word, "If Timothy come, see that he be with you without fear." "Do not frighten him," he seems to say. "Make his task as easy as possible by undergirding him with your sympathy and your prayers. Only thus will he be able to give you his best."

Then I think that Timothy was not only timid in appearing before an audience and in doing the ordinary work of

81

a Christian minister, but I think he was naturally afraid of
the actual dangers that a minister had to face in preaching
the gospel to that pagan world. He knew something of the
sufferings of Paul, his father in the faith. Perhaps the first
time he ever saw him he was little better than a dead man
because of the stoning he had received. He knew that Paul
had again and again known the agony of the whipping post.
Timothy knew that such might happen to him also. Thus
facing up to the task of being a Christian minister in that day
was hard enough for one who was naturally courageous.
How doubly hard it was for a timid man such as Timothy!

A second handicap that Timothy had was a kind of fatal
incapacity to grow up. It is really a privilege to be a youth,
but to stay that way is not so good. To the mind of Paul,
Timothy was always a boy. He addressed him as "my child."
In his letter to the Corinthians, after he has warned them
against frightening Timothy, he adds, "Let no man therefore despise him." Or, "Let no man think slightingly of
him." Ten years later, when he sent Timothy a personal
letter, he wrote, "Let no man despise thy youth"—that is,
"Don't allow folks to look down on you because you are
young. Don't let people push you aside saying, 'Oh, he's just
a boy!' "

Just why Timothy was unable to grow up we cannot say.
Perhaps he was not nearly so youthful in reality as Paul
thought him. Perhaps the fact that his early training was
so exclusively in the hands of two doting women had something to do with it. Don't misunderstand me. I am not
slandering these two good women. Thank God for them both.
But in all probability they babied Timothy a little too much,
with the result that he found life a good deal harder because

of this pampering and because he had been so securely tied to his mother's apron strings. Anyway, he was handicapped by the fact that his extreme youthfulness made it hard for some to take him seriously.

Finally, Timothy was not physically strong. As some would say, he enjoyed poor health. The context would indicate that Timothy's sickness was due in part to the fact that he was too strenuous with himself. He perhaps thought meanly of his body. He perhaps looked upon it as an enemy to his soul rather than its friend. For many years certain saints thought it very wise to crucify the flesh in order to free the spirit. But it so happens that body and soul are closely united. A healthy body is thus a great help toward a healthy soul.

This ought to be remembered by all of us, especially by the minister. I know there are those who seem to think that if the minister is sickly, it adds somewhat to his piety. But such is in reality not the case. A weak body may be a terrible liability. It may be such a handicap as to cause us to pity ourselves and shrink from the battle and refuse to face up to life. Of course, rightly used, it may be one of those "all things" that work together for our good. But there is no doubt that Timothy, being timid and boyish and sickly, found it especially hard to face up to life.

This is evidenced, not simply by our text, but by repeated urgings on the part of his father in the faith. "Neglect not the gift that is in thee," Paul writes. He knows that Timothy has a gift even as you and I. He knows that all that is necessary in order for Timothy to allow his gift to go to waste is for him to neglect it by refusing to face up to life. Again he urges, "Stir up the gift of God that is within thee"—

83

better translated, "Rekindle the gift of God that is within thee." "Timothy," Paul implies, "you are about to allow your fire to go out. Keep it burning by accepting your share of suffering. Remember that God hath not given us a spirit of cowardice but of power and of love and of sanity."

"Till I come," writes this same faithful friend, "give attendance to reading." This, of course, may refer to the public reading of the Word. But it is capable of another meaning. Paul is saying, "Don't let anything keep you from being a student. 'Study to show thyself approved unto God.'" That is a needed word for every one of us. It is especially needed by every teacher in the church school. What a travesty on the importance of the work you are undertaking when you come before your class, whether of three or of thirty, without any preparation. It is supremely important for the minister. Were I in the pew, I could easily forgive my pastor for the flattest of failures provided he had done his best. But I should find it hard to forgive him if he persisted in appearing in the pulpit hoping for some happy inspiration to atone for his being too lazy to prepare.

IV

"As a good soldier of Christ Jesus, accept your share of suffering." What did this timid, boyish, sickly preacher do with that stirring word? He did not resent it. He did not tell himself: "It is well enough for Paul to talk like that. He has never known the meaning of fear. He has a fighting heart. It is easy for him to stand up to life, but not for me. For me it is impossible." No, in spite of all his handicaps, he took Paul seriously and won.

1. Facing up to his share of the hardships, he won over

himself. Being timid and sickly, it would have been very easy for him to have been an introvert. It would have been exceedingly easy for him to have excused himself and to have rotted down in self-pity. Sickness and suffering do not always result in unselfishness. It may make us the most self-centered of people. But Timothy used his to his enrichment rather than to his impoverishment. Thus when Paul wrote to the church at Philippi he could write after this fashion: "I have no man like him who will naturally care for you. So many others seek their own ends, but he unselfishly seeks the glory of his Lord." Timothy knew how to love unselfishly. Paul with a great longing tugging at his heart writes of how he yearns to see him, being mindful of his tears, that he might be filled with joy. In facing up to Paul's appeal, he conquered himself.

2. In facing up to Paul's appeal, Timothy conquered his laziness—his tendency to shirk, to take the easy way. Paul could write of him, "He worketh the work of the Lord as I also do."

"Timothy, aren't you a bit ill today?"

"Yes," he answers, "but not ill enough to quit work."

As I walked the streets of Edinburgh, Scotland, I thought again and again of Robert Louis Stevenson. He had a frail, tortured body, as did Timothy; but he still worked, worked with a heroism that makes our hearts glow to this day. Even so, in spite of his handicap, Timothy was a worker.

3. Finally, as Timothy faced up to life, he conquered his timidity. He overcame his fears. One day he had a letter from his old friend. I think as he read it he had to stop more than once to wipe away the tears in order to see. As he read not only what was written but what was between the lines, the

letter ran somewhat as follows: "Dear Timothy, I write to inform you that I would be alone today but for the presence of my good friend Doctor Luke. Demas has forsaken me, while others that are dear to me I have sent to man difficult posts on far-flung fronts. I want you to come to me. When you come, please bring my old cloak that I left at the home of Carpus in Troas. My cell is a bit cold. Also bring my books and parchments. Do your best to come before winter. The Lord give mercy to the house of Onesiphorous, for he often refreshed me and was not ashamed of my chain."

This man Onesiphorous, of the ugly name and the beautiful soul, must have been well worth knowing. I am sorry I can't give you a better view of his face. Paul said, "He oft refreshed me." When fair-weather friends came to Rome, they were afraid to visit the great apostle. He was in jail, and to be his friend was dangerous. But Onesiphorous was a beautiful exception. He sought him out diligently. As Paul writes of him in the past tense, the chances are that he paid for his devotion with his life. The apostle seems to be saying as much to Timothy. He is warning him delicately, "If you come, Timothy, it might cost you suffering, it might cost you imprisonment, it might cost you your life." But he urges him to come, partly because he needs him, but far more because he is eager for Timothy to gain the victory that comes from the conquest of fear.

What, then, did this timid, sickly, young man do with this appeal? He did the thing he was desperately afraid to do. He made his way to Rome. He put himself in the power of bloody-handed Nero. He and Luke and Mark were three friends that in all probability were present when Paul said his final farewell and went out to pay the last full measure of devotion. It would seem that Timothy himself was then arrested and put in prison. At least, the writer of the letter to the Hebrews tells us a little later of his release. Thus Timothy had come to possess the finest type of courage, a courage that led him to defy his fears by doing his duty even when it brought him a pallid face and trembling knees.

Now whatever you may be doing with your life, whatever I may be doing with mine, I think we admire the way this timid young man of the long ago defied his handicaps to face up to life. Therefore, I challenge your heart and mine with the same words that strengthened him—"As a good soldier of Christ Jesus, accept your share of suffering." God has given you a gift that is unique. You can do something for him that nobody else can do. If you face up to life in his strength, he will enable you in the finest sense to save your own life. What is better still, he will enable you to steady, strengthen, and save others. Therefore, "as a good soldier of Christ Jesus accept your share of suffering."

VIII

I'D AVOID BEING HALF-BAKED

"Ephraim is a cake not turned."

HOSEA 7:8

I

WHAT IS WRONG WITH EPHRAIM? HE IS NOT CHARGED with any crime. He is not accused of being either selfish or cowardly or crooked. The one accusation against him is that he is half-baked. He is like a cake that is well done, even perhaps burned on one side, but entirely raw on the other. Therefore, in spite of the fact that he has good stuff in him, he does not arrive. In spite of the fact that there is no fault to be found with his capacity, he is for all practical purposes useless.

We can see at once that Ephraim is by no means a unique character. We meet men of his kind every day. They are wanting in symmetry. They are not balanced. They are lacking in a certain well-roundedness. They have too much of one thing and too little of another. They are creatures who go to extremes. They are often burned to a crisp on one side but utterly raw on the other. They remind us, even as does Ephraim, of a cake not turned.

Some of us are out of balance physically. I had a good friend who served through the first World War. When it was over, before he was mustered out, he was asked to pose for a statue of the typical American soldier. Whether he accepted the invitation or not I do not know. But the reason the invitation was given was that he was so symmetrical. He had an almost perfect body. He did not have lovely eyes and no teeth. He did not have one arm as strong as that of a giant and the other as weak as that of a child. He did not have one foot of ordinary size and the other big enough to wear one of those seven-league boots. He was chosen because he was symmetrically developed.

Just as we need symmetry of body, we need also symmetry of mind. An unbalanced mind is a calamity. When it is too pronounced, it sends its victim to the madhouse. Then we need to keep the balance between the physical and mental. To have a tremendously strong body with a weak mind is not appealing. A hackneyed phrase has crept into our language that describes a certain type of girl. We call her "beautiful but dumb!" Sometimes her beauty of body serves only to accentuate her dumbness, so that her possible charm becomes more of a liability than an asset. The dinosaur had a tremendously strong body, but he lacked a brain to match. He was half-baked. Therefore, the centuries rubbed him out. We need a balanced mind in a balanced body.

Then we need to be symmetrical, not only in body and mind, but also in heart. To have much heart and too little mind is often to be so soft as to do as much harm as good. But to have a keen mind with little heart is merely to be a human icicle. Such may do effective work in many directions, but they have no friends. We may respect them, but we never love them. Often they become a menace to society. The truth of the matter is that the greatest threat to our civilization today grows out of the fact that our hearts have not kept pace with our heads. Therefore, our amazing genius, which should have been used for the making of instruments for the enriching of life, has been too largely used for the making of implements of destruction. Thus, as individuals and as nations, we are half-baked. We, as Ephraim, may be described as a cake not turned.

II

What, then, is the prophet urging? He is urging that individually and socially we should be well-rounded. He is recommending that type of culture which Arnold described as the "harmonious expansion of all our powers." He is urging us to avoid extremes. He is recommending what the ancients called the golden mean. We are to seek to be balanced personalities.

This is what the Latin poet Ovid was teaching in his story of Daedalus and Icarus. These two, father and son, were exiled on the island of Crete. They sought a way of making their escape. Since they had no ship, their only hope was to fly. The father, being an inventive and practical man, made two pairs of wings. This he did by the use of feathers and wax. When the wings were made, both father and son learned to fly. At last, when they had developed sufficient skill for their adventure, the great day came for their escape. Then the father gave his son final instructions. "Don't fly too low," he urged. "Otherwise enemies from the ground will get you, and you will fail to win your goal. But neither must you fly too high. If you do, the sun will melt the wax and your wings will fall apart, and you will fall with them and thus fail of your purpose." Then he added, "You will go safest in the middle."

Fortified by this word of wisdom, the son set out on his journey. For awhile all went well. Then he began to glory in his newly found powers. Equipped with these wings, he felt able for anything. Therefore, in spite of his father's warning, he climbed higher and higher. Too late he realized that the sun had got in its deadly work. The wax was melted. The wings came apart, and he fell to his death. This was the case not because his adventure was impossible. His father won his way to safety with similar equipment. It was the case not because Icarus refused to make any effort. It was the case because he refused to steer a balanced course. He forgot his father's wise advice that he would go safest in the middle.

What is this poet seeking to teach? He is not merely giving advice to our politicians. No more is he urging us to play the role of the halfhearted or of the colorless neutral. There are those who seek to avoid taking sides on a moral issue at all. Then, even when forced to take sides, these often seek to be neither very good nor very bad. They thus become about the most unattractive and useless individuals in the world. "I hate folks," says the author of Psalm 119, "I hate folks who are half and half." So do we—so does everybody! Such a type was extremely disgusting to Jesus himself. He said, "Because thou art lukewarm, and neither cold nor hot, I will spew thee out my mouth." This word of the poet is certainly not a warning against desperate earnestness.

What then, I repeat, does Ovid mean? He means that we shall become our best by avoiding extremes, by developing harmoniously. We can understand the good sense of this when we realize the fact that many of our worst vices are only virtues pushed too far. Take economy, for instance. It is wise to conserve our wealth. It is foolish to be reckless and wasteful in the use of money. Money that I have earned represents myself. It is a part of my time. It is a bit of my personality. It is condensed energy. It is pent-up power. It is power that I can release for the helping or the hurting of men. I have no right to be careless in its use. Wastefulness is not only silly; it is wicked. The accusation against the Prodigal Son was that he wasted his substance with riotous living.

The other day I saw a soldier doing his best to give his money away. He was all but forcing it into the hands of strangers. Why was this the case? It was not because he was wise. It was rather because he was drunk. To be indifferent to any kind of value is not sensible. To waste is not wise, but stupid; not big, but little. It is only the small that waste. Big things never do. This is a big world on which we live. But it is not a wasteful world. It has never wasted one single drop of water or one single grain of sand or one single weed or flower. When Jesus fed the multitude, he said, "Gather up the fragments that remain, that nothing be lost." Even our God has nothing to throw away.

But while it is wise and right to be economical, there are those who push their economies too far. There are those who, refusing to make money their servant, allow it to become their master. Beginning by a sane saving, they end in an insane miserliness. Of all the degrading loves that we let into our hearts, there is none more deadly than the love of money. It has a way of blinding our eyes to life's finer values. It has a way of killing our better selves. It has a way of electrogalvanizing us—soul, mind, and body—so that we drop into our coffins at the end of the day with a clank like the ring of a coin. To practice economy is a fine virtue; to push it too far is a most ugly vice.

Then what a beautiful virtue is courage! Of all the virtues, I think it is the most universally admired. It has been admired in all ages. The cave man admired it. The most cultivated of moderns admires it no less. It is admired by the old and by the young, by those in the Occident and by those in the Orient. It is admired by the most learned and by the most ignorant. It is a virtue that is so important that it calls for a grudging respect even in the most unlovely. It is so important that its absence is hard to forgive even in the otherwise lovely.

But as beautiful as courage is, it can be pushed too far. When pushed too far, it becomes recklessness. Now no man has a right to be reckless. Sometimes we claim for certain individuals that they are entirely without fear. Generally speaking, that is not true. It would not be any great compliment if it were. An ordinary bulldog knows little of fear, but he is not for that reason the highest type of hero. When one is so courageous as to be reckless, he endangers his own life as well as that of others. No risk is too great to take for a worthy cause. But to risk the priceless treasure of life for a trifle or for nothing is at once foolish and wicked. Recklessness is only the fine virtue of courage pushed too far.

III

Since we desire to be well rounded, where shall we turn to find one who not only can serve as our model but who can also give us the power for the reaching of our goal? The answer to that question I find in Jesus Christ our Lord. He was the most perfectly balanced, the most beautifully symmetrical character that this world has ever known. If we fail to recognize that, it is because we have never given ourselves a chance really to know him. Let us look, then, at some of the marks of perfect balance and poise that we find in him whom many of us are happy to call our Lord and Master.

1. How tender he was! What a roomy heart he had! There were many outcasts among his people, but not one of them was beyond his interest and love. One day when a group of cruel men threw a soiled rag of womanhood at his feet, demanding that she be stoned, he took her part. He treated her with the same tender courtesy that he would have shown to the purest of the pure. When mothers came into his presence with their babies in their arms, there was always trouble. These little fellows insisted on climbing out of mother's lap and climbing up into the lap of Jesus. It was written of him, "A bruised reed shall he not break and the smoking flax shall he not quench." He was and is the Christ of the battered and bruised and broken folks.

But while he was unspeakably tender, he was never soft. While he was gentle, he was never maudlin. Though his were the kindliest eyes that ever looked upon men, that does not mean that he went about with a smile of approval for every one whom he met. While he commended some with words that thrill us to this day, there were others he rebuked. While he approved some, there were others that he scourged with the sword of his mouth. While there were some for whom he could find no words too tender, there were others for whom he could find no words too bitter. He called them a generation of snakes and wondered in the heat of his moral indignation how they could escape the damnation of hell. He was unspeakably gentle and tender, but he was also unspeakably firm and strong.

2. He was a man of amazing self-control. There are some folks who pride themselves on being high-tempered. They seem to think that it is a mark of strength that they have little self-control. They are as easy to set off as a powder magazine. In a fit of temper they slam doors, kick over chairs, give themselves the luxury of violent language. There was none of that about Jesus. He was tantalized and contradicted as few ever have been. On one occasion without any sufficient provocation a man slapped his face. But Jesus kept his temper and refused to hit back. One of his dearest friends, himself a passionate and fiery man, writing of him forty years after the crucifixion, calls attention to the characteristic in him that I am sure impressed him most. This is what he wrote: "When he was reviled, he reviled not again."

But the fact that Jesus was a man of perfect self-control does not mean that he was a man of ice. A hotter heart than his never beat in a human bosom. At times he fairly blazed with hot anger. One day he went into a church where there was a man with a withered hand. He found that the religious leaders of the day were more concerned in keeping their petty rules than in giving this man help. We read, therefore, that he looked round upon them with anger. It was an anger that scorched and blistered and burned. Those who saw it never forgot it. His was the anger of the "terrible meek." Such anger differs from ours conspicuously in this respect: We usually get angry when we are personally insulted. We can blaze when one interferes with our rights.

95

But Jesus never grew angry over wrongs done to himself but only over wrongs inflicted upon others. It was when weakness was imposed upon by strength, it was when right was outraged by might, that he blazed. It was then that he became fiery-eyed and defiant. Here, then, is a man of hottest passion, but of perfect self-control.

3. Then Jesus was a deeply serious man. He was tremendously in earnest. He was so in earnest that his friends read in his tired face one day the interpretation of a passage of Scripture that they had never understood before. "The zeal of thine house hath eaten me up." He was genuinely in earnest and so deeply serious that he was called "a man of sorrows and acquainted with grief." He was so serious that there were times when his face was wet with tears. There were times that he sobbed as only the brokenhearted sob. Naturally many have come to think of him as one who could never laugh and whose face was seldom·if ever lighted by a smile.

But this is very far from telling the whole story. In spite of his seriousness—and because of this fact!—he was the most joyful of men. The artists have done Jesus a great injustice by picturing him as one whose life was one long sob. He did sob, but he also sang. He could laugh. He was possessed of a delicious sense of humor, as any reader of the Gospels can see. In fact, he was so glad that many of his day who looked on religion as a bit of a kill-joy did not think that Jesus was religious at all. He was the most earnest of men and yet the most joyful. These two should always go together. The flippant seldom truly laugh, however many laughing noises they make. Those too serious to laugh generally major on minors. Our balanced Christ could both laugh and weep.

4. He was the world's greatest dreamer. One day he locked up his little carpenter shop in Nazareth and went out with no lesser hope than the conquest of the whole world. But while he dreamed he did more. He could "dream and not make dreams his master, and think and not make thoughts his aim." If he was the world's supreme dreamer, he was also the world's supreme realist. Of all the practical men that ever set foot on the planet, he was the most practical. Men and nations must accept his way because life won't work in any other. To turn from him is to face toward chaos and death. In him the idealist and the realist were perfectly blended.

5. He was the most vital of men, with a passionate love of life. It was his abounding vitality that was part of the secret of the spell that he cast over men. Turn the pages of the New Testament and see how often men came to him to ask him about life. He tells us plainly that he did not lose his life. Instead, he gave it. Superior force did not wrench it from his grudging hands and clinging fingers. "No man taketh it from me, but I lay it down of myself." He was passionately in love with life, but he was glad to die in order to accomplish the will of God.

6. Finally, Jesus was deeply religious. No man was ever more so. But he was never sanctimonious. He never paraded his piety. He never struck an attitude or assumed an unctious tone. In fact, no other man ever hated mere pious talk as he did. Hypocrisy was his pet horror. One day a peddler of pious twaddle broke in on his message with this fine word: "Blessed is he that shall eat bread in the kingdom of God!"

But Jesus failed to show the slightest appreciation. Instead, he at once proceeded to tell the story of a "certain man who made a great supper, and bade many: And sent his servant at supper time to say to them that were bidden, Come; for all things are now ready. And they all with one consent began to make excuse." Thus was Jesus reminding this seemingly earnest man that he did not really desire a place at the feast of the fullness of life. He only wished to have a reputation for such a desire. Jesus had the hatred of an intensely sincere man for such pretense. The sanctimonious parader finds nothing but rebuke in his presence.

His hatred of pretense was so intense because his love for reality was so profound. Religion for him meant a deep and clear realization of God. How real God was to him! How constantly he enjoyed his companionship! "He that hath sent me is with me: the Father hath not left me alone; for I do always those things that please him." He was a strong Man, the strongest of the strong; but he never trusted in his own strength. He declared, "I can of mine own self do nothing." He lived his life upheld by a mighty faith in a fatherly God. When he hung on the cross, the worst that his enemies could say of him was, "He trusted in God." The last word that fell from his lips was a prayer that he had learned at his mother's knee: "Father, into thy hands I commend my spirit." He was the most religious of men, yet utterly free of any touch of sanctimoniousness.

Here, then, is One at whose feet we may sit and learn. Here is a well-rounded Man. Here is a Man of perfect symmetry. He offers to be your Friend and mine. Some of you as soldiers and sailors are going out to strange and trying experiences. But you do not have to go alone. Our Christ is eager and able to go with you all of the way. If you give him a chance, he will enable you to feel in the most trying situation that the Eternal God is your dwelling place and that underneath are the everlasting arms. Thus undergirding you, he will also increasingly enable you to possess a poised and balanced personality akin to his own.

IX

I'D LEARN TO FORGIVE

"So likewise shall my heavenly Father do also unto you, if ye from your hearts forgive not every one his brother their trespasses."

MATTHEW 18:35

No series of sermons, whether to young or old, would be in any sense complete without a message on the important matter of forgiveness. Here is an impressive word from the lips of Jesus himself. At first glance this word sounds somewhat harsh and forbidding. It seems more like a threat than an invitation to privilege. But such is not in reality the case. In spite of its seeming harshness it contains a most helpful and fundamental truth that is in harmony with the whole of the New Testament. The Master is here saying in substance what his servant Paul wrote to the Ephesians, "Be ye kind one to another, tenderhearted, forgiving one another even as God for Christ's sake hath forgiven you." There is nothing more important, if we are to master the art of living, than that we learn to forgive.

I

What is it for us to forgive one another from our hearts, as Jesus enjoins in this text? Such forgiveness means something far bigger than merely to ignore those who wrong or despitefully use us. Recently a professing Christian was emphasizing the fact that she refused to resent a slight on the part of her neighbor. This she did, according to her own explanation, because she considered the source. Now, if by considering the source we mean that we judge another kindly because he has not had an adequate chance, that is all to the good. But if we mean that we refuse to resent because of our contempt for the one who wrought this injury, then such an attitude is the farthest possible from Christian forgiveness. To forgive is something far bigger than to ignore.

Then the forgiveness that Jesus enjoins goes deeper than a refusal to exact an eye for an eye and a tooth for a tooth. It is far more than refusing to exchange slander for slander or blow for blow. I may refuse to get even with you for an injury you have done me and yet not be forgiving in the least. I may refuse even to utter against you an unkind criticism and yet fall vastly short of what Jesus meant by forgiveness. What then, I repeat, is forgiveness?

For us to forgive is to have the same attitude toward our enemies that God has toward his. That is a high standard, I know. But it is the one set by Jesus himself. How, then, does God treat his enemies? He exercises toward all of them an active and aggressive good will. It might be very impressive to see the field of a wicked man parched by drouth while the field of his righteous neighbor was golden with wheat. But God makes no such distinction between his foes and his friends. "He maketh his sun to rise on the evil and on the good, and sendeth rain on the just and on the unjust."

As God treats his enemies, so are we to treat ours. We are not only to refuse to hit back in a spirit of revenge, but we are to bless them that curse us and pray for them that despitefully use and persecute us. It is only by doing this that we can show ourselves kinfolk with God. It is only by our meeting ill will with good will that we can save ourselves from bringing bitter disappointment to our Lord. "If ye love them which love you, what reward have ye?—And if ye salute your brethren only, what do ye more than others?" In other words, we are to have the same attitude toward our enemies that God has toward his.

Not only does God show kindness both to friend and foe, but he offers forgiveness to both. He offers this forgiveness to every one regardless of the greatness of his sin. He offers this forgiveness persistently and constantly. He offers this forgiveness constantly regardless of how long the sinner may persist in his sin. God is always forgiving all men. The difference between the saint and the sinner is not that one is forgiven while the other is not. It is rather in the fact that the saint accepts his forgiveness while the sinner refuses to accept. God's forgiveness is constantly offered to both.

Even so it must be with ourselves. We are to forgive every injury, however great. We are to forgive the one who has wronged us regardless of how great that wrong may be and regardless of how long the wrongdoer may have persisted in his wrongdoing. That is what Jesus is saying in the story of which our text is a part. Simon came with a question, "How oft shall my brother sin against me, and I forgive him—till seven times?" Simon thought he was being exceedingly liberal, but Jesus answered, "I say not unto thee, Until seven times; but, Until seventy times seven." By this he meant that, as there is no limit to the forgiveness of God, so there must be no limit to our forgiveness. Our attitude to our fellows must be constantly one of forgiveness.

Finally, when God forgives he takes the sinner back into his fellowship and into confidence once more. Forgiveness, for God, means reconciliation. It means that God and the sinner have become friends. It means that God forgets an ugly past and treats the offender as if he had never gone wrong. That is what forgiveness must mean for us. It is, therefore, more than ignoring, more than refusing to strike back. It is to meet evil with good. It is, so far as in us lies, to change our foes into our friends. Forgiveness, therefore, is something tremendously important and Godlike.

II

Why are we thus to forgive?

1. We are to forgive for our own sakes. There are certain evils that are deadly foes to personality. There are evils that all psychologists agree tear life apart. These evils are four in number. Jesus pointed them out many centuries ago. The first is self-centeredness. To be self-centered is to be in a real sense self-destructive. It is to refuse in the fullest sense to live. "Whosoever shall seek to save his life shall lose it." That is true not simply in prayer meeting, but in the home, on the street, everywhere.

The second deadly foe to personality is worry. To face life with an attitude of fear instead of faith is to do ourselves an irreparable injury.

A third personality poison is a sense of guilt. Lady Macbeth was a woman of strong will. While she was awake she kept some measure of self-control by sheer determination, but when sleep had relaxed her watchfulness she gave expression to the anguish that tortured her. Her sense of guilt so tore her apart that she had to sob, "Out, out damned spot."

The fourth deadly foe to personality is hate. I have known a few very intelligent haters. I have known some who had got on and made what men call a success. But I have yet to meet a happy and wholesome hater. I am thinking now of a man who spent years getting even with one of his fellows who had injured him. He believed in the truth of the saying "Revenge is sweet." But now that he has won, his hard, tortured face does not look to me in the least like that of a man who is tasting sweetness. On the contrary, he gives the impression of one who is tasting the very bitterness of hell. We ought to refuse to hate just as we refuse to take bichloride of mercury. Both are deadly poisons.

2. We ought to forgive, not only because of the injury that hate works to the hater, but also because of the injury that it works to others. If I hate you, I might do you some positive harm. I might even become so embittered and enraged that I would take your life. If I should refuse to go to such extremes, even then I might speak a critical word that would so injure your reputation as to cause you great pain. Roger Chillingsworth, in Hawthorne's immortal story, was a great hater. He hung upon the track of his victim like a bloodhound until that victim was forced to confess his shame to the world. Hate often results in aggressive harm to the hated.

But in order for my hate to hurt others, it is not necessary that I seek to do the one I hate the slightest harm. Even though I refuse to give any aggressive expression to my hate, the very fact that I am a hater makes me cheat my loved ones, my friends, my church, the whole world. This it does because of the injury that it works to me personally. By refusing, therefore, to forgive, I not only hurt myself but I help to lower the moral and spiritual temperature of the world.

Then I should forgive because it is only by forgiving, or by being willing to forgive, that I can receive the forgiveness of God. This fact Jesus emphasizes again and again. This is how he taught us to pray, "Forgive us our debts"— in what measure?—"as we forgive our debtors." In fact, according to Jesus, the one condition for our being forgiven is that we forgive others. "For if ye forgive men their trespasses, your heavenly Father will also forgive you. But if ye forgive not men their trespasses, neither will your Father forgive your trespasses." This also is what he says in our text: "So likewise shall my heavenly Father do also unto you, if ye from your hearts forgive not every one his brother their trespasses."

On the surface this sounds arbitrary. But of course such is not the case. God will not forgive the unforgiving because he cannot. When God forgives, he takes us into his friendship. In that friendship, our natures are renewed. We become new creatures. We come to see our fellows through his eyes. But God cannot give us new hearts of love if we insist on clinging to our old hates. God can no more forgive the unforgiving than he can make life to be death at one and the same time. We ought therefore to forgive for our own sakes and for the sake of others. We ought to forgive because there is no other door by which we can enter into the fellowship of God.

III

How, then, can we forgive?

Years ago a friend of mine preached a sermon on forgiveness. At the close of the service, a prominent woman invited the minister home with her to dinner. When the dinner was over and the two were seated in the parlor, this cultivated woman turned to the minister with these words. "You said this morning that there could be no forgiveness for us unless we too should forgive. Did you mean that?" When the minister answered in the affirmative, when he declared that the conditions were not his but God's, when he assured her further that these conditions were not arbitrary but existed in the very nature of things, the woman, at once hopeless and resentful, declared with emphasis, "Then that leaves me out. There was a man at church this morning who did me such an injury that I can neither forgive nor forget."

Now there are doubtless some of you who can sympathize with this woman. Believe me, it is not always easy to forgive. It is not easy even for God. If it is not easy for our Lord, it is certainly not easy for you and me. Humanly speaking, there are times when we find it impossible to forgive. Yet this is a lesson that we must learn. There is simply no Christian life for those who cannot forgive. Blessed, therefore, are those who learn in youth how to be forgiving. How then can we, in spite of our tendency to strike back, learn to be forgiving? I am going to offer four suggestions which I have found helpful:

1. It may help us to forgive if we remember, as stated above, that, while hate may hurt others, it strikes its deadliest blow at the hater. There is good sense in cultivating

flowers, but why cultivate a nettle such as hate that can do nothing for me but torture me by its sting?

2. We may find it easier to forgive if we compel ourselves to act constantly toward our enemies as if they were our friends. We can act our way into forgiveness, generally speaking, more readily than we forgive our way into right acting.

3. I find it easier to forgive when I remember how greatly I have been forgiven. This is where the creditor in our story went wrong. He owed his lord ten thousand talents. Now that does not sound like such a great sum to us. We are accustomed to think of money in terms of our national debt. But in the time of Jesus this was a perfectly impossible sum. Taxes in Palestine were high, yet the annual revenue from the five provinces of that country was only eight hundred talents. A man possessed of ten thousand talents could have hired ten million soldiers, had so many been available, to fight for him a whole year. This man's indebtedness, therefore, was so great that to pay it was an impossibility.

Now his king, not willing to lose the entire sum, ordered the debtor to be sold, together with his wife and children, that he might collect at least a small fraction of the money that was due him. But in desperation the poor fellow threw himself at his lord's feet and prayed, "Have patience with me and I will pay thee all." Of course, the king knew that he could never make good his prayer. Yet he forgave him, not for hope of gain but out of sheer pity. Thus forgiven, the once desperate man came out from the king's presence with a new hope in his heart and a new light in his face. Life for him through this forgiveness had taken on a new departure.

But soon something took place that plunged this forgiven

man into an utter blackout. He had not gone far from his master's presence before all the light suddenly went out of his face. In bitterness he was gripping a cowering fellow servant by the throat and roaring at him, "Pay me that seventeen dollars you owe me." This poor chap hastened to fling himself upon his face and to pray, "Have patience with me and I will pay thee all." It was exactly the same prayer that he himself had prayed only a few moments ago. There was, however, this great difference: this fellow servant might have paid his debt, for it was a paltry sum, while his own debt was beyond payment. But, though greatly forgiven, he refused to forgive. Instead, he actually had his debtor cast into prison.

Soon the news of this heartless conduct spread abroad. It was told, first to his fellow servants, then to the king. When his lord heard it he called him and said: "I forgave thee all that debt, because thou desiredst me: shouldst not thou also have had compassion on thy fellow servant, even as I had pity on thee? And his lord . . . delivered him to the tormentors." Why so? There was nothing arbitrary in it. His torment did not come from his lord, but at his own hands. By his unbrotherly conduct he became the bondslave of his own hate. His tragedy was that, though he had been greatly forgiven, he himself refused to forgive. The fact that we have been forgiven so much ought to make it possible for us to forgive.

4. Finally, if we are to forgive we must have the help of God. Our Lord does not expect us to forgive in our own strength. He only asks that we be willing to forgive. He asks even less than this: he asks that we be willing to be made willing. When we will for ourselves what he wills for

us, the impossible becomes possible. The man of the world can imitate many Christian virtues. He can be clean, generous, and courageous. But to love one's enemies, to possess always toward all men a forgiving spirit, that he cannot imitate. We reach that high goal only when we give God a chance to help us.

Here is a story from the life of a British soldier. It was related, I think, by Francis C. Stifles. This soldier, a young officer, is writing to a mother in Germany. The letter was something like this: "My dear Madam: In the course of a commando raid on a French village, it became my duty to kill your son. I write earnestly to ask your forgiveness, for I am a Christian. I hope after the war is over that I may see you and talk with you face to face."

Months later the young officer received this answer: "My dear Captain: I find it in my heart to forgive you, even you, who killed my son; for I too am a Christian. If we are living after the war is over, I hope you will come to Germany to visit me, that you may take the place in my home, if only for a time, of my son whom you killed." How beautiful! But nobody can work a miracle like that but God.

X

I'D LIVE POSITIVELY

"When the unclean spirit is gone out of a man, he walketh through dry places, seeking rest, and findeth none. Then he saith, I will return into my house from whence I came out; and when he is come, he findeth it empty, swept, and garnished. Then goeth he, and taketh with himself seven other spirits more wicked than himself, and they enter in and dwell there: and the last state of that man is worse than the first."

MATTHEW 12:43-45

HERE IS A GRAPHIC PICTURE FROM THE LIPS OF THE MASter himself. It is the story of a man's battle with evil. This man has become aware of a hated guest that is homing in the house of his heart and has determined at any cost to be rid of that guest. This unwelcome guest is unclean, while the man himself longs to be clean. The presence of this evil tenant means a certain kind of bondage, while the man who is giving it hospitality longs to be free. Therefore, he rises in his might and expels this unwelcome guest from his life. But instead of finding the freedom that he expected, he ended by finding a greater bondage. All his efforts at victorious living were futile. "The last state of that man is worse than the first."

I

Why did he fail?

He did not fail through indifference to the evil that possessed him. He did not fail because he had no interest in the living of a better and cleaner life. He was keenly interested in being free of his unwelcome guest. He longed for what he conceived to be the good life. That is true to a greater or lesser degree with all of us. However trifling and indifferent we may seem, there are times when even the most indifferent of us looks wistfully toward the heights and longs to climb. There are times when every one of us says, consciously or unconsciously,

> "Oh, for the man to rise in me
> That the man I am may cease to be!"

If this man did not fail because he was indifferent to the good life, no more did he fail for lack of effort. He did not simply wish to be free of his unwelcome guest; he willed that freedom. He willed it so intensely that, at God only knows what cost to himself, he showed this foul guest the door. Having expelled him, he sought to remove all the stains that his evil presence had brought. The once unclean house was swept and garnished.

If the man did not fail for lack of earnestness nor for lack of effort, no more did he fail because the task to which he set himself was impossible. It is true that he failed finally to get rid of his hated guest, but that does not mean that his failure was inevitable. On the contrary, his failure was utterly needless. Countless thousands have found themselves in his pathetic plight and have gloriously won. If there is a promise that is emphasized by our Lord, it is the promise of victory. We do not have to be the host of evil. It is our privilege to be the host of our Lord himself. "Behold, I stand at the door and knock: if any man hear my voice and open the door, I will come in."

Why, then, I repeat, did this earnest and struggling man fail? He failed, as so many do, because he used a wrong technique. When he decided to live a good life, as we should say, to become a Christian, he fixed his mind on the evil to be expelled rather than on the good that was to take its place. He focused his attention on the tares rather than upon the wheat. He sought to be negatively good. He believed that he could win by merely cleansing the house of his heart of its evil. Therefore, he rose up against his hated guest and expelled him. Having attained an empty house, he thought he had won. That was his fatal blunder.

II

Now what is wrong with trying to be good merely by fighting evil? This method is a failure for at least three reasons.

1. Emptiness of evil, however complete, is no equivalent for goodness. Mere harmlessness is never holiness. To make the casting out of evil an end in itself is to forget the true goal. What is God seeking in your life and mine? What was the farmer seeking when he sowed good seed in his field? He was seeking wheat. The servants made the mistake of thinking that his primary purpose was to be rid of tares. But this was not the case. This farmer, putting the raising of

wheat first, was willing to let the tares grow rather than run the risk of spoiling the wheat. He might have destroyed the tares utterly. But if he had destroyed the wheat at the same time, he would have won only a barren waste. Thus he would have missed the whole purpose for which the field was cultivated and the wheat sowed.

When I was a boy on the farm, we had certain uplands that we had to clean up every spring. This ground was especially fruitful in sassafras sprouts. These we had to destroy. Our purpose in so doing was not that the field might be bare but that the corn might have a better chance to grow. This indicates God's purpose in dealing with us. This is the meaning of every so-called sacrifice that he asks us to make. He is seeking positive goodness in your life and mine. When, therefore, he asks us to give up this or that evil, it is not that our hands and hearts may be empty, but that they may be full of positive goodness.

"Moses when he was come to years refused to be called the son of Pharaoh's daughter." We honor this man. Here he stood with his foot on the steps of the throne of the mightiest nation in the world, yet he renounced that throne. What was the good of it? No good at all if he had merely renounced it, then folded his hands and done nothing. In fact, such a renunciation would have been positive sin, for he was a man of vast ability and might have made a great pharaoh. We see the beauty of his renunciation when we read the rest of the sentence, "Moses when he was come to years refused to be called the son of Pharaoh's daughter, choosing rather to suffer affliction with the people of God." He gave up the privileges of a throne that he might have the greater privilege of bringing about the birth of a nation.

Every renunciation that God calls upon us to make is only a means to an end. "Be not drunk with wine, wherein is excess." Why not? Is not there a thrill in getting drunk? I am told that there is. A few drinks of liquor makes the timid man bold and the modest girl brazen. It makes the poor man feel rich. Multitudes drink in order to forget their sordid selves, the treadmill monotony of life. They seek to feel a momentary release. But such intoxication refuses to last. It leaves those who indulge in it with an ill head and an aching heart. Like a flash of lightning on a dark night, it leaves only a greater blackness when it is gone.

Yet Paul, in warning us against getting drunk, does not claim that even being a total abstainer will make a man a saint. Herein lies the stupidity of those who claim that the prohibitionist is trying to make folks religious by legal enactment. The prohibitionist recognizes the drunken man as a menace. He is trying to protect society. While no Christian will get drunk, no man is a saint because he does not get drunk. Thus, when Paul says, "Be not drunk with wine, wherein is excess," he goes on to add, "but be filled with the Spirit." Here is a thrill that will last. Here is an experience that will make life so full that all evil as well as all lesser good will be crowded out. But mere emptiness of evil is never an end in itself. There is little good in escaping Egypt with its bondage if we merely wander in the wilderness and fail to reach Canaan with its freedom. To be harmless is not to be holy.

2. Not only does emptiness fall short of positive goodness, but it is in itself a sin. So wrote James with sanest common sense: "To him that knoweth to do good and doeth it not, to him it is sin." This means that no amount of "don'ts" can

make a Christian. If merely to do no evil would make one good, then it would be possible to make a St. John out of a wax figure or a Susannah Wesley out of a rag doll. Adding up "don'ts" is just like adding up a column of ciphers: the sum always is nothing.

Not only is emptiness sin, but Jesus looked upon it as a most dangerous and subtle type of sin. It is easy to see why this is the case. The man who gets drunk and shoots up a town knows that he is wrong. But the one that does no positive harm often looks upon himself as a choice saint and wonders why he fails to grow wings. This is true of the negatively good, both within and without the Church. Some of the most critical and pharisaical people with whom I have had to do have been professing Christians who were constantly priding themselves on the thousand-and-one sins that they did not commit. This they did while they were often unable to point to a single positive good that they did. How often I have asked some man to become a Christian, only to be answered, "I am not so bad. I don't do anything wrong."

But what is it to do wrong? One of the most dangerous and damning of all sins is merely to do nothing. Therefore, Jesus warns against this danger more than against any other. In his parables of judgment his rebuke is never for the man who has done some bold and aggressive wrong; it is rather for the one who has failed to do the bold and aggressive right. Why did the man of one talent lose his treasure while he himself was flung out into the night? It was certainly not because he had wasted his substance with riotous living. He had not squandered his money only to stand before his lord empty-handed. He had rather refused to use it at all. He had kept it laid up in a napkin. The fig tree was ripe for destruction, not because it bore poisonous fruit, but because it bore none at all. The five foolish girls had the door shut in their faces, not because they were antagonistic to the bridegroom, but because they had no oil. The most insidious and dangerous of sins is to have come and grown and gone and never to have known the privilege of taking an aggressive stand for the right.

3. Not only is emptiness passive sin; it leads almost inevitably to open and aggressive sin. When this earnest man bestirred himself against the evil passion that homed in his heart, he drove it out. Then he thought that his work was done. He had a house that was clean and empty. But the trouble with an empty house is that it invites an occupant. Its very emptiness flouts a sign "To let" in the face of every passing demon. The truth is that no house can be empty. If you will not entertain a good guest, then you will entertain an evil one. Of all the difficult tasks there is none quite so difficult as being good without being good for something.

The futility of this impossible achievement may be read in countless tragic failures. Take Samson, for instance. We read that this iron man judged Israel for twenty years. As long as he remained on the job, he was true to his vow of dedication to God. But after a score of years he decided on a holiday. He decided to take that holiday, not among his friends, but among his enemies. He went down to Gaza. Here without any fine love to fill his heart, he fell in love with Delilah. That guilty love began at once to feel for the secret of his power. Soon he was a blinded slave in the prison house. Leaving off the positive right, he ended by doing the positive wrong. Thus every empty house invites a tenant.

III

If we are to win, we must live positively.

1. This is true in the realm of the physical. How, for instance, shall we enjoy good health? Some folks make the mistake of seeking to win by focusing their attention on disease. They are constantly feeling their pulse, and looking at their tongue, and consulting some physician. As a consequence, they are also constantly enjoying bad health. In order to be well, something more is necessary than merely getting rid of disease. A distinguished physician told me a few years ago that he was curing cancer, but he said the patient always died. I have no reason to doubt his word. Death will cure any disease. "That is an ugly cough you have," said the manager of the morgue. "Yes," replied his visitor, "but any of these chaps lying about on these slabs would be glad to have it." Certainly! A cough may be bad, but it is not so bad as death. Merely to kill disease is not enough.

The only positive remedy against sickness is health. The late Dr. Cabot of Boston, in a book on *What a Minister Ought to Know About Sickness,* tells of a chap who was killed by a car in front of his clinic. Dr. Cabot declared that an autopsy performed on this body indicated that, while the man was in good health, he was yet afflicted with at least three deadly diseases. He had sclerosis of the liver, but nature had rerouted the blood so as to take care of this. He had tuberculosis, but nature had enclosed the deadly germs in little prison houses so that they could no longer do their destructive work. I am not sure about the third. Nature, by building up the patient, had given him health in spite of the disease; but a mere absence of disease does not positively guarantee health. It might only mean death.

2. It is by the positive truth that we are to drive out error and correct false faiths. There are those who are ready to lay hold on any new ism that comes along. This is generally the case because they have a vacuum on the inside. But how are we going to fight these errors? One way is to denounce them, tear them into shreds, show how silly they are. Go up to your friend with his little tallow-dip and say, "That is a futile light," and then blow it out and leave him in the dark! No, the method of denunciation will not work. It never has. It never will. The denouncer almost always stirs up more snakes than he kills.

How, then, shall we proceed? We must realize that the only foe of darkness is light. The only sure antagonist of error is truth. How the early saints demonstrated this! They went out into a hard and forbidding world where polytheism was old and entrenched and respectable. How slow would have been their progress if they had begun by denouncing Jupiter for a tyrant and Venus for a bit of a harlot, and on through the list. Instead, they went out to proclaim Jesus Christ, both by their lips and by their lives. Therefore, when those pagans saw him as the "fairest of ten thousand and the One altogether lovely," they forgot their false gods as we forget the stars at the coming of the sunrise.

3. Here is the secret of a victorious Church. Now and then solicitous saints rise up in defense of the Church. They seek to protect it. The Church at times seeks to protect itself. Such a course always ends in failure. The church that seeks to save its life will lose it, just as the individual. The only way a church can save itself is by giving itself. The only way

that it can be strong is not by digging in and standing a siege but by going to the attack.

Here again we learn from the Early Church. These saints never allowed themselves to be put on the defensive. In the present war we were for months at a terrible disadvantage because our enemies were on the offensive while we were on the defensive. I used to coach football. I was not much of a coach, but I at least knew this much—that my team would never make a touchdown while the other team carried the ball. When Paul was before Agrippa, he was asked to defend himself. But he soon forgot himself as he made an attack on the citadel of Agrippa's soul. The only way for the Church to win is to be positive and aggressive.

4. It is only by being positive that we can achieve a better world. We are hoping and praying for an abiding peace. Nothing could be more important than this. Jesus pronounces a blessing on the peacemaker. But we must realize that peace is something far bigger and better than the mere cessation of war. The cannon may cease to thunder and the soldiers may lay down their arms without our having any real peace. So it was at the end of the last war. I was in Europe a little while after the armistice. While men were no longer fighting, there was no real peace. On the contrary, there were times when I could feel the breath of hate about me as if it had been a living presence. To make peace is not a passive something, but a positive. It is to displace war with its opposite. It is to substitute confidence for fear, co-operation for antagonism, good will for ill will. Rome at its tyrannous worst held "a fretful world in awe." She compelled it to be at peace, but her gift was the peace of death. If we are to have a better world, we must make a positive peace.

5. Finally, this is a way of victory for the individual. How unfortunate it is that so many think of Christian living in terms of the negative. Ask the average man outside the Church to become a Christian, and too often he will think of your invitation in terms of what he will have to give up instead of what he is to receive. But always the emphasis of Jesus is on what we are to receive. The big reason for the giving up of anything is that we may receive something better. The key word of Christianity always is "Receive ye." It is used over and over again. For instance, when John sought to tell of the amazing difference that knowing Jesus had made in his own life and in the lives of his fellow Christians, he did not point to what they had given up, but to what they had received. "Of his fullness have all we received," he explains joyfully.

Then since being a Christian is to receive our Lord, it is also to become workers together with him. This is the road to victory. The one sure way to keep our hands from the unclean and forbidden is to give them fully to the doing of the beautiful and the worth-while. Here, for instance, is a gifted young man, Nehemiah by name, who is undertaking an almost impossible task. He is seeking to rebuild the capital of his shattered and broken nation. He is being persistently hampered by foes within and without. The voice of temptation calls to him constantly. But he goes on his way with serene courage. What is his secret? Hear it in his own words: "I am doing a great work, so that I cannot come down." His work under God was his life preserver. The same may be the case for you and me. "This I say then, Walk in the Spirit, and ye shall not fulfill the lust of the flesh." The only way to live victoriously is to live positively.

XI

I'D START AGAIN

"Rise, let us be going."

MATTHEW 26:46

OUR TEXT IS A PART OF THE STORY OF THE CROSS. JESUS has just gone into the Garden of Gethsemane to prepare himself for the awful ordeal of Calvary. Arrived within these familiar haunts, he takes with him, to share his sorrow, the three friends who belong to the inner circle, Peter, James, and John. These men had been with him when he went into the home of Jairus to change death into life. When a little later he went into the Mount of Transfiguration, again he took these chosen three. Now great privilege always involves great responsibility. Therefore, when the Master comes to this hour of supreme testing, he takes with him Peter, James, and John.

I

Why did he take these three men?

1. He took them for their own good. He invited them that in his fellowship, which is the fellowship of prayer, they

might prepare themselves for the awful ordeal that was ahead. He knew, as we learn sooner or later, that to go to our task prayerless is to go powerless. This was their opportunity to get ready for the terrible test that, unknown to themselves, was soon to shake them to the very foundations of their being. In Bunyan's immortal story, you remember how Christian won his way to the Palace Beautiful, whose open door was welcome and whose atmosphere was peace. Then when he had rested and was ready to resume his journey, he was led through the armory chamber. Here he had an opportunity to select the weapons of defense and offense that he would need as he braved the hardships of his pilgrimage. Here was the helmet of salvation, the breastplate of righteousness, the sword of the Spirit. It was his privilege so to arm himself that he would be more than conqueror in his conflict. That is what this hour of watching with Jesus was to mean to these three friends.

2. Then Jesus invited them to share with him this hour of prayer that they might gather strength, not only for themselves, but for their fellows as well. Their weaker brothers were also to undergo sore trials. They would need some strong human arm upon which to lean. Peter, James, and John might have been as towers of strength to them. If cowardice is exceedingly contagious, courage is equally so. No man can stand in his place and be true in the hour of testing without making every other man stronger. These friends of the inner circle were therefore invited to this hour that they might strengthen themselves and thus have something to share with their needy fellows.

3. Finally, Jesus invited these friends to be with him in this agony because he needed them. Our Lord was thoroughly

human. There were therefore times when he leaned heavily upon human help, even as you and I. His heart at this time was hungering for the fellowship, the sympathy, and the understanding of his friends. He shrank from passing through his terrible ordeal alone. Loneliness is at times almost unbearable for a sensitive soul, and Jesus was exceedingly sensitive. Listen to his own words: "Behold the hour cometh, yea, is now come, that ye shall be scattered, every man to his own, and shall leave me alone." Jesus would never have said that but for his deep dread of loneliness.

Now loneliness, as you know, is of two kinds. First, there is physical loneliness. There is the loneliness that we experience when we are separated from our fellows by sundering seas or dividing mountains. There is the loneliness of solitary confinement such as some prisoners know. Charles Reade tells of a certain prisoner who was shut up in a dark dungeon alone. He felt his reason slipping. In his desperation he tore the buttons from his clothes and flung them on the floor, and then sought to pick them up and count them in an effort to keep from going stark mad.

I know that there is a loneliness that has healing in it.

> "There is a pleasure in the pathless woods,
> In the society where none dwells."

But such loneliness becomes torture if we have to endure it too long. Here is a voice to that effect:

> "O solitude! where are the charms
> That sages have seen in thy face?
> Better dwell in the midst of alarms,
> Than reign in this horrible place.
>
> "I am out of humanity's reach,
> I must finish my journey alone,

Never hear the sweet music of speech,
  I start at the sound of my own.

"The beasts that roam over the plain,
  My form with indifference see,
They are so unacquainted with man,
  Their tameness is shocking to me."

Jesus in his hour of trial dreaded to be alone physically; hence he took with him Peter, James, and John.

But the supreme dread of the Master was of the loneliness that is of the spirit. Our Lord was lonely, as truly great souls so often are, because he saw a vision that others did not see. He was dreaming great dreams that others did not share. He deeply longed to have somebody near him as he faced the cross who might at least have a glimmering understanding of the agony of it all. Thus, because of the needs of these three disciples, because of the needs of their fellow disciples, and because of his own great need Jesus invited these friends to watch with him.

II

Theirs was a great opportunity—an opportunity to help themselves, to help others, and to help their Master. What did they do with this big chance? They threw it away. Instead of watching, they went to sleep. What a human story it is! We have all passed through kindred experiences. We have all made similar failures. I read in the book of Isaiah of one of whom it is written, "He shall not fail." When I read that, I knew the author was not talking about me. I knew he was not talking about any of my friends, even the bravest and the best. We have all failed in some measure. In fact, the book of our life story has a way of opening at places kept by blighted flowers of privilege and of opportunity.

When Jesus came seeking the consolation of their watchful sympathy, he found them fast asleep. He asked Peter a question that seems literally soaked in tears of disappointment. "What, could ye not watch with me one hour?" Then they bestir themselves, try with bitter shame to do better only to fall asleep again. At last Jesus comes with this strange word: "Sleep on now and take your rest: behold the hour is at hand, and the Son of man is betrayed into the hands of sinners."

What does Jesus mean by that word—"Sleep on now and take your rest?" Scholars differ in their translation of this passage. If the King James and the American Revised Versions are correct, it would seem, as Frederick W. Robertson suggests, that the Master is seeking to bring these failing friends face to face with their unalterable, irrevocable past. "You have slept," he seems to say, "and thus have missed your opportunity. You may sleep on now so far as that opportunity is concerned. You may sleep on 'till the stars are old and the sun is cold, and the leaves of judgment unfold', but you will no more have missed your chance than you have missed it already. So sleep on now and take your rest."

Here, then, is a most startling fact—day by day you and I come face to face with privileges and opportunities of which we must take advantage or we will miss them forever. Every hour brings its gifts and lays them at our feet. We must utilize these gifts, or that hour will gather them in its strong hands and slip through the gate of the past and be gone forever. Though we may pound at that gate with bruised fists, though we may tamper at its lock with bleeding fingers, we can never get back the hour that is gone. The sunrise hour of this morning is as completely beyond our reach as the first hour that ever burst in splendor upon this world.

While I was pastor in Fort Worth years ago I went one day to catch a train for a speaking engagement. Contrary to my custom, I reached the station twenty minutes ahead of time. Having bought my ticket, I seated myself in front of the door where I could see the train when it came in. Then I took a book from my grip and began to read. It was an interesting book. The next time I looked up it was past train time. That fact did not worry me in the least. I was sure that the train was late. Therefore, I simply went over to the agent and asked, "How late is the train this morning?"

"It has been gone five minutes," he answered. Now this agent was not inclined to preach. But had he been so, he might have said, "Read on now and finish your book. Read on till you have waded through all the manuscripts of the past. Read on till you have finished the books that are yet hidden in the bosom of the centuries. Even then you will no more have missed your train than you have missed it already. So read on and finish your book!"

One day I was making a trip by rail over a road that for a brief hour gave the passengers the privilege of a view of gorgeous mountain scenery. Now I confess a real love for the mountains and the hills. I was born in a rugged country. I have never been able to get my heart out of the hills, nor the hills out of my heart. When I asked the conductor how long it would be before we would come in sight of the mountains, he answered that it would be about an hour. Being drowsy I decided to take a little nap. So I fell asleep! A few minutes later, as I thought, I awoke. Again I asked how long it would be until we could see the mountains. "We passed them over two hours ago," was the answer. Here again, had the conductor been disposed, he might have said: "Sleep on now and take your rest. Sleep on till the very mountains are level with the plains. Even so you will no more have missed your chance than you have missed it already." "I will do better next time," we are fond of saying. But so many things have no next time!

III

Is this all that Jesus has to say to those who have failed? If so, we are all in a tragic plight, because we have all failed in some measure. When Paul declares, "There is no difference, all have sinned," generally speaking, we do not smite our breasts and say, "Woe is me." But when he adds the further declaration that we have come short, that strikes closer home. Our consciousness of sin may be rather vague. Even so, few of us will claim that we have always been in when duty called. We are ready to confess, however great our attainments, that we have not measured up to our best. All of us have failed in somewhat.

Now what, I repeat, does our Lord have to say to such failures as these three friends, to such failures as we? This is his heartening word, "Rise, let us be going." How heartening! He does not merely say, "Get up and go, but you will have to go alone. I refuse to cast my lot with such shameful failures." He says, rather, "Let *us* be going." He is still eager to go forward with us, regardless of the ugliness of our failures and regardless of how long we have persisted in making them.

A gentleman said in my presence some time ago, "No man

ever lets me down but once." A father said recently, speaking of a son who had disappointed and shamed him, "He has made his own bed, let him lie on it." Thank God, our Lord is not like that. He has a way of treating sin that is unique. Some of us are so conscious of our soiled yesterdays that we are in danger of losing both today and tomorrow. Some of us allow the memories of past failures to paralyze us and to keep us from trying any more. But Jesus urges us to turn our backs upon our sinful past. Paul is passing on what he had learned from Jesus himself when he urges us to forget the things that are behind. The one something in the universe that God forgets is your sin and mine. What he forgets we have a right to forget. You may be sure that the Christ who expects us to forgive until seventy times seven will not expect less of himself.

Here, then, is the gospel of a second chance. It is a gospel of a thousand, yea, of endless chances. No failure need ever be final. No fall need end in tragedy. The only disaster that is without remedy is to quit trying. The difference between those who have gone down in defeat and those who have triumphed is not that one sometimes failed while the other never did. The real difference is that one accepted his failure as final, told himself there was no hope, while the other dared to start again. Simon Peter's life might have ended as tragically as that of Judas had he not dared to start anew. The life of Judas might have ended triumphantly. Indeed, he might have been the most amazing miracle of the New Testament had he only dared to make a new start. The most painful wound that this traitor inflicted upon his Lord was not his kiss of betrayal but his failure to trust him enough to make a new start.

Life for the best of us, generally speaking, is not a constant progress upward. It is rather a constant making of new beginnings after we have failed. One of the most effective ministers of a score of years ago told this story out of his own experience: One day a boy came to the country school he attended with an old one-string fiddle tucked under his arm. George looked upon that fiddle with eager eyes. When his friend showed a willingness to sell it, George bought it, paying for it his sling, his marbles—in fact, all the treasures he had. When school was out he carried his prize home, telling his family that he had made up his mind to be a violinist. But soon his enthusiasm cooled, his patience became threadbare. When his brother, Jim, offered to take the fiddle off his hands, he sold it to him and felt a sense of relief that he had got so well out of an embarrassing situation.

Then George watched Jim take the instrument in hand. He expected him soon to grow discouraged, but Jim was made of stronger stuff. He sawed on that fiddle till the family chased him into the yard and from the yard into the wood lot. Then one day Jim came home to inform the family, as they sat about the evening meal, that he could play five tunes. After supper his father asked him to give a concert. When Jim had complied, his father said never a word. But the next day he went to the city to bring home to Jim a beautiful new violin. And Jim became so proficient that George declared he had been charmed by his music times without number.

A few years later George was converted and felt called to the ministry. He was to preach in the little country church that was attended by his kinfolks and his neighbors. When the great day came, George stood up before the congregation of familiar faces and read his text. But his sermon went from him. He read it a second time and then a third time, but he could not say a word. Then in shame and desperation he sat down, buried his face in his hands, and sobbed. A kindly old layman dismissed the congregation and they all went home. At last George looked out from behind the pulpit to find that the church was empty. Then he slipped home and went up to his little room in the attic, where he flung himself across the bed and vowed he would never try again.

As he thus accepted his failure an inner voice seemed to say to him, "George, you remember the time when you bought that one-string fiddle and determined that you would learn to play? Don't you remember how after a little while you gave it up in disgust declaring that nobody could play such an instrument? And don't you remember that your brother, Jim, took that same instrument and learned to play so well that his father believed in him and bought him a new violin? And don't you know that today he is an accomplished violinist? You failed where he succeeded. This you did because you quit. Now you have been called to preach. But because you have made one failure you are going to throw your chance away."

"Then," George said, "I pulled myself together and made a solemn vow: 'Lord, I have only a one-string violin of ability, but if you will give me another chance I will do my best with what I have.' " What was the outcome? That one-string fiddle became by the help of God a marvelous orchestra that thrilled and moved and won thousands. Indeed, few ministers of his day were more useful than George R. Stuart. He won because he dared to start again. There is only one failure without remedy—to quit trying. So to all who have failed, I bring this invitation from my Lord, "Rise, let us be going."

XII

I'D BE SENSIBLE

"Now, everyone who listens to these words of mine and acts upon them will be like a sensible man."

MATTHEW 7:24 (MOFFATT)

THESE WORDS COME AT THE END OF WHAT WE KNOW AS the Sermon on the Mount. Whether these sayings of Jesus were uttered as a single address or were collected in the present form matters nothing. Whenever they were uttered we may be sure that Matthew rightly records the reaction of those who heard them. When the congregation broke up and went away in twos and threes the people said one to another: "This preacher is different. I never heard anybody just like him before. There is a ring of certainty in his voice that is as refreshing as it is unique. He surely seems to have a first-hand knowledge of that about which he is talking. He speaks as one having authority and not as the scribes."

In thus declaring that Jesus spoke with authority these ancient hearers were using words that sound to us almost timid. Not only did Jesus speak with authority, but with superb audacity. He dared to tell his hearers that their destiny depended absolutely on the attitude they took toward his teaching. What he said to these hearers of the long ago he has said to the ages. What he said to them he says to us of today. Emphatically he affirms that to refuse to act upon his teaching is to meet disaster individually and socially. On the other hand, he declares that if we do take his words seriously we shall find life both individually and socially. Not even God himself could make a more daring claim than this. Yet the experience of the individual as well as the experience of the race utters to these words an emphatic "Amen."

In this beautiful story of which our text is a part Jesus makes four very obvious assertions:

I

He affirms that all of us are builders. When our Lord speaks of building he can speak with especial authority because that was perhaps his own field. The fact that Jesus was a carpenter means, no doubt, that he did something more than make chairs and tables and farm utensils. He also built houses. Even if he did not actually build them himself, he knew about building. More than once in his own neighborhood had he seen substantial-looking houses swept away for lack of solid foundations. He had seen other houses weather those same storms because they had in them the strength of the solid rock upon which they were founded.

Now it is the contention of Jesus that, while all of us are builders, we do not all build in the same fashion. There are those who build wisely. They act like sensible men. There are others who build foolishly. It is not their wickedness that is emphasized, but their silliness. But, whether wisely or foolishly, all of us are building. Of course, the house that we build is none other than our own character. That means that day by day we are becoming certain types of men and women. What we are today depends upon how well we builded yesterday. What we shall be tomorrow will depend upon how well we build today.

What we have builded thus far is naturally of great importance. That is the case because what we have builded determines what we are. But, while what we are is of vast importance, what we are becoming is still more important. When I was a boy on the farm, we raised various kinds of domestic animals and birds. For instance, we raised horses and hogs, cattle and sheep. We also raised chickens and ducks, geese and turkeys. At least, we tried to raise turkeys. If you have ever experimented with this bird, you know that there is nothing that a young turkey likes quite so well as to die. But we were quite successful with other birds, especially with the geese. Now if you had the good fortune to grow up on the farm and thus to become acquainted personally with the goose family, you will have to confess that a gosling is a beautiful creature. In fact, its beauty is superb. But, while confessing the loveliness of this young creature, I could never grow vastly enthusiastic about it. This was the case because I always had it in the back of my mind that if it kept on the way that it was then going it would surely one day become a goose. This gosling was building, but it was building for nothing better than goosehood.

On the other hand, if you had been cleaning up your home some morning toward the end of winter and had come upon an ugly wormlike something anchored upon your window sill, if you had set yourself to tear this bit of ugliness from its anchorage and in disgust to throw it into the fire, I might have protested. "That," I would have said, "is the cocoon of an emperor moth. It is quite ugly now, but in spite of its present ugliness it is on the way to marvelous beauty. Give it a chance, then one day there will be a knocking inside that uncouth prison and a guest will come to visit you on wings more colorful than the rainbow. That creature is headed toward spring. Be patient with it therefore, not because of what it is now, but because of what it is becoming." Wisely or foolishly all of us are building our own house of life. That is the first assertion of this story.

II

The second fact that Jesus affirms is that the house I build, as well as the house you build, is to be tested. There will be gracious and sunny days for all of us, thank God. But there will also be days when black clouds will scud across our skies and fierce tempests will beat upon us. However sheltered my house may be, however sheltered yours may be, the tempest is sure to break upon us sooner or later. This is the case because God has put us in a realm of choices. That means that by all of us decisions must be made. For all of us the roads fork every day. That is just another way of saying that temptation is a universal experience.

Since the roads fork every day, this testing of the house of life is a process. The winds of temptation toy with more or less violence with your house every day. What you do in the face of these lesser storms is of vast importance. In fact, what you do when the great tempests break upon you is generally determined by what you have done with the lesser tempests with which you have fought day by day. If in your commonplace days you have suffered defeat, if under the small tempests you have made tame surrenders, that is likely to cause you to make a great surrender when the big hour of crisis comes. If day by day you have told yourself and others little white lies, been guilty of petty insincerities, that course is likely to issue one day in a colossal lie and in a ruinous collapse.

But while testing is an everyday experience, there comes to practically all of us an hour of tremendous crisis. There come to all of us storms whose issues will be a bracing triumph or a tearful tragedy. How did Judas come to his fall? He was certainly not created for the mean role that he played. He was not born a traitor. Luke tells us plainly that he became a traitor. How? Why? In spite of the love of his Master, he came to be guilty of petty deceptions, small dishonesties. These grew day by day. At last the heavy storm broke upon him; he went to pieces and betrayed his Lord with a kiss.

All of us, Jesus affirms, are builders. Whether we build wisely or foolishly, all our buildings are being constantly tested. All of them come sooner or later to a supreme test whose issues are a matter of life and death.

III

The third assertion that Jesus makes is that, while storms break upon every life, the effect of the storm is not for all of us the same. Here were two houses that Jesus knew. Perhaps they were in sight of each other. During the sunny days there was little to choose between them. The house of the foolish builder looked just as strong and abiding as that of the sensible man who had builded wisely. Then suddenly the rains came, the floods rose, the winds raged. The wild storm was on. It beat upon both houses. But while one stood firmly upon its solid foundation, the other was swept away, an utter wreck.

Some time ago I drove by a forest where a storm had recently raged. In other days the passer-by could see two magnificent trees standing close together in that forest. One of these trees looked just as strong as the other. But now one had crashed, while the other seemed to stand all the taller and the more erect because of the wreckage that was all about it. It was not the storm that made the difference between these two trees. The difference was there before the storm came. The storm simply made the difference manifest. While it brought ruin to one tree, it brought greater strength to the other.

Thus it is with the tempests that break upon men. The fact that one wins through while the other crashes is not to be explained by saying that while the tempest broke upon one the other lived all his life under clear skies. The truth is that it is not the fierceness of the tempest that decides our fate; it is what the tempest finds in us. The same fellowship that changed fluctuating Simon into a rock of Christlike character, that made fanatical John into an apostle of love, changed Judas into a traitor. We are all builders. The characters we build must be tested by the storm. But the issues of the test will not be the same. The tempest that is the minister of life to one will be to another the minister of death.

IV

Finally, Jesus tells us what is to be the decisive factor that will determine whether the house we have builded will stand or fall. He affirms that our destinies are not matters of chance. He is sure that we do not have to be the victims of circumstance. When he stood at the end of life's journey he claimed with a calm assurance that he had overcome, that he had lived victoriously. He had met the storms of life, but his house had remained firm upon its foundation. "A kindred victory," he affirms, "is within your reach." How is this victory to be won?

Listen to the answer in Jesus' own words: "Everyone who listens to these words of mine and acts upon them will be like a sensible man who built his house on rock. . . . And everyone that listens to these words of mine and does not act upon them will be like a stupid man, who built his house on sand." There was a difference in the reaction of these two men that made all the difference between success and failure, victory and defeat, life and death. What was that difference?

To begin, it was not that one listened to the words of Jesus while the other turned away and refused to listen. There are those, of course, who miss the best because they have never had an opportunity to hear the gospel message. But this story indicates that both these men were hearers. Yet listening is not enough. Our own experiences have taught us again and again that we may hear to no purpose. In fact, one of the major dangers of the constant churchgoer is the tendency to believe that by the mere act of listening he has measured up to his responsibility.

Not only is listening not enough, but it is not enough to listen with approval. It is not even enough to listen with such approval that we receive the message without question. This becomes evident when we realize that some of the most cranky and cantankerous people that we have known along the way have been churchmen who were intensely proud of their orthodoxy. There are those who fancy that they are saints because they vow that they believe every word of the Bible from cover to cover. But such faith may be entirely fruitless. James tells us that the devils themselves believe but they are not transformed by their faith, nor do they seek to transform others—they only shudder. It is not enough therefore either to hear or to believe the sayings of Jesus. We must go beyond that.

What, then, is the one essential? What is it that makes the difference between life and death for these two men and for all mankind. The answer is action. "Everyone who listens to these words of mine and acts upon them will be like a sensible man." In thus making action or obedience the essential condition of victorious living Jesus is altogether sane and reasonable. What he says is not arbitrary. It is true in the nature of things. It is only as we act that we come to knowledge in any department of life. It is not enough for one to believe that bread will satisfy hunger and that water will slake thirst. Before that faith will result in any good, it must be acted upon. To refuse to act is to starve. When I was a farmer I came to believe beyond a peradventure that if I planted corn and cultivated the crop I would reap corn when the harvest time came. I was sure also that if I sowed wheat I would reap a harvest of wheat. I am just as sure of the rightness of my position today as I was then. But in spite of this fact, I am not expecting to reap either wheat or corn during the coming harvest. This is the case, not because the law of sowing and reaping has changed, but because I am not acting on the knowledge I have. I am no longer farming.

A lovely girl promised to marry me a good many years ago. Her promise might have gone for nothing and I might now be a cranky old bachelor had I not acted upon that promise. When just out of my teens I decided to apply for a scholarship in our oldest university. It looked like a long, slim chance, but I determined to take it. So I sent in my application. Then one night I went over to our little village for the mail. There was only one thin letter. It was addressed to me. I noticed that it came from Cambridge, Massachusetts. When I opened it, it read as follows: "Your application for a scholarship at Harvard University has been favorably considered. Please report at Lower Massachusetts Hall, September 28, at 10:00 A.M."

That was to me very thrilling. But, having read that letter, I might have said to myself sadly: "What a pity that I do not dare take advantage of this generous offer. But if I should make the long journey to Cambridge I would have to borrow the money to pay my traveling expenses. If when I reached my destination the authorities were to fail to live up to their promise, then I should certainly be in an embarrassing situation both financially and otherwise." Thus I might have heaved a sigh and missed my chance. Instead, I was too wise to take such a silly course. I said to myself: "I will certainly be there. If there is only one man present in Lower Massachusetts Hall on September 28 at 10:00 A.M., I am going to be that man as surely as I am alive and able to stand." I not only believed, but I was determined to act. By thus acting on the word of the authorities at Harvard University I received my scholarship.

It is acting on the words of Jesus that counts for the individual and for the world. What is the supreme tragedy of the bleeding nations of earth at this moment? Why are we so destroying each other that we seem as a world eager to commit suicide? Fundamentally, it is because we have never acted upon the words of Jesus. The nations that are leaders in this strife have for many years been labeled Christian. But in too many respects those nations have been Christian in name only. They have heard the sayings of Jesus about brotherhood, about the necessity of loving one another, about the penalty of taking the sword; but they have refused to act upon these words. Thus refusing, they have found the result just what Jesus said it would be—disaster. It does not take a wise man to see that the course that is being persistently pursued by the so-called Christian nations is not only wicked, it is foolish—foolish to the point of insanity.

What do you propose to do with the words of Jesus? Do you mean to applaud them, to look at them as lovely dreams, as beautiful ideals and nothing more? If so, you can promise yourself little today or tomorrow but tragedy. This is the case because these words are true. They are true as the law of sowing and reaping is true. They are true as the law of gravity is true. The man who assumes that the law of gravity will operate at one time but not at another may be wicked, but he is above all else silly. The same is true of the man who refuses to act upon the words of Jesus. Wicked he may be, but above all else he is playing the fool. The only wisdom is to take Jesus seriously. It is thus and only thus that we can build both for time and for eternity. May God help us thus to be sensible.

XIII

I'D HAVE A GOOD TIME

"Always be joyful."

I THESSALONIANS 5:17 (SMITH-GOODSPEED)

ALWAYS BE JOYFUL. HAVE A GOOD TIME ALL THE TIME."
That sounds like a big order in a world like ours.
Surely the man who said this must have been born on the
sunny side of the street. Surely he must have led a sheltered
life, free from the slings and arrows of outrageous fortune
that are the lot of so many of his fellows. Certainly no rude
winds ever blew upon him. No wild tempests ever shook
their brutal fists in his face. We feel that "along the cool,
sequestered vale of life" he must have kept the noiseless
tenor of his way. Therefore, from his place of security, while
reclining upon pillows of ease, he calls out to his fellows,
"Always be joyful."

But it so happens that this man who calls on all and sundry
to have a good time was not in reality a son of good fortune
at all. Once he had had an assured position in his church, but
he gave that up to cast his lot in with a new and unpopular
movement that was loved by a few and hated by many. If

he ever had any wealth, he had lost that. As for a sheltered life, he knew nothing of it. Instead, he knew what it was to be constantly on the march. He had known shipwreck. He had been stoned and left for dead. He knew the inside of many a Roman prison. He had been to the whipping post so many times that his whole back was little more than a scar. He tells us frankly that he had suffered the loss of all things. Therefore, it is not a son of good fortune but a strenuous son of battle who calls to us this word, "Always be joyful."

I

This word from Paul is more than a bit of good advice. It is a command—a very roomy command. Look at its content.

1. It speaks home to a universal longing. "Always be joyful. Have a good time." That is just what we all desire to do. However far we may be missing the experience of joy now, all of us are longing and hoping for it. Nobody desires to find life like a trudge through a desert. Nobody wishes his days to be one long series of yawns. All of us desire a bit of song and a bit of laughter. We are eager for some golden sunlight to illuminate our pathway. Everybody desires to have a good time. I think such desire is God-given. He has put it in our hearts for a high and holy purpose. Thus many of the endless sensible and silly things that we are doing day by day have as their goal the winning of a good time. Those who waste their substance with riotous living, those also who invest themselves in earnest and helpful and respectable living, are all eager to be joyous. This command speaks home to a universal longing.

2. This command also indicates a universal possibility.

"Rejoice evermore." Who is to do that? Not merely those who have attained certain material treasures, not the famous and the successful alone, but all of us. This joy that the apostle commands is for everybody. It is for the weak and for the strong, for the cultured and the uncultured, for the successful and for the failures, for the rich and for the poor. It is for those who have made their way into the limelight; it is no less for those who must live their lives in obscurity. There are many prizes you and I cannot attain, but here is one of vast worth that is within reach of all of us. We may all have a good time.

Not only does this command speak home to a universal longing and to a universal possibility, but also to a universal obligation. Since everybody can have a good time, everybody ought to have a good time. Joy is a great privilege, but it is more than a privilege—it is a duty. We Christians are prone to forget this. There are those who seem convinced that sadness is a mark of piety. Their theme song is,

> "This world is but a desert drear,
> Heaven is my home."

But to go through life looking like an incarnate sob is more than a misfortune—it is a sin. Gallant-hearted Robert Louis Stevenson, whose earthly pilgrimage was one long battle with pain, recognized this. Therefore, he looked upon happiness as more than a privilege. It was a positive duty. That is what he means when he prays:

> "If I have faltered more or less
> In my great task of happiness;
> . . . .

Lord, thy most pointed pleasure take
And stab my spirit broad awake."

It is everybody's duty to have a good time.

II

Why is every one of us under obligations to be joyful?

1. This is the case in the first place because it is only as we are joyful that we can come to our best. It is the only way that we can be our best physically. A wise man said long ago, "A merry heart doeth good like a medicine." Moffatt translates this, "A glad heart helps and heals." That is not mere preaching. That is sober truth, as every physician can testify. Here are two men in the same hospital afflicted to the same degree with the same disease, but one of them is cheerful and joyous while the other is cheerless. Which is likely to get well the quicker? The joyous man of course. "A glad heart helps and heals."

"One of the most deadly diseases from which men suffer," a certain physician said to his minister the other day, "is one that our medicines cannot reach."

"What is that?" the minister questioned. "Cancer?"

"No," came the answer, "it is boredom."

That is true. Thousands die every year, not because they have some deadly physical malady, but because they have lost their zest. These refuse to go on living because they feel that they have nothing left for which to live. They know nothing of the cheerful heart that helps and heals. "More than half the beds in our hospitals," said a noted physician recently, "are occupied by men and women whose sickness is not physical but mental." It is our duty to have a good time because this is the only way that we can be our best physically.

Then, just as cheerfulness is conducive to physical health, so it is to health of the spirit. No man can enjoy good spiritual health who is gloomy and despondent and joyless. "The joy of the Lord," said a writer of the long ago, "is your strength." Certainly! It is your strength for wholesome living. It is your strength for resisting those germs of spiritual sickness that we call temptation. The only sure way to shut out the worst is by the inviting in of the best. We may try to drive out darkness with a club, but our effort will end in failure. This is the case because the only effective foe of darkness is light. The only effective way to resist the call of the world is by the positive possession of something better than the world can give. The joy of the Lord is our strength for resisting temptation.

Ulysses discovered this principle in the long ago. One menace of the sea in his day were the sirens. They sang so beautifully that the ships that passed their way were lured to their destruction. To prevent this, sea captains were accustomed to have the ears of their sailors stuffed with wool so that they could hear nothing. But when Ulysses passed that dangerous way, he took Orpheus with him—Orpheus, who could play so beautifully that it was said that the very rocks and trees were unable to resist the spell of his music. Then, when the sirens began to sing and the prows of the vessels began to turn toward those death-haunted shores, Ulysses ordered Orpheus to strike his harp. This done, the ships sailed on to their desired haven, for the music on board was so much sweeter than the music of the sirens that the lure of their song lost its charm. Thus it is in possession of a positive joy that we are to resist temptation. "This I say then, Walk in the Spirit, and ye shall not fulfill the lusts of the flesh."

2. It is a positive duty of every one of us to be joyous because in no other way can we discharge our obligations to our fellows. Robert G. Ingersoll asked a question bitterly one day to the effect that since cowardice and sickness were contagious, why should not their opposites be also. Now it so happens that that is exactly the case. I have seen one member of a family spread gloom over the whole household. Even so, one member can help every member to have a good time. You have no more right to rob me of my joy than you do to rob me of my money. We ought to be joyful because, if we are not, we are apt to commit the sin of being a kill-joy.

Not only should everybody be joyous because we cheat our fellows otherwise, but because by our gladness we help and hearten. Then we ought to be joyous in order to commend our religion to others. The joy of the Lord is our strength, not only for resisting temptation; it is also very largely our strength for the winning of others to the Lord whom we serve. If we are gloomy, if we are persistently complaining, if we are everlastingly talking and acting as if our Father in heaven had died, leaving us eternally bankrupt, then it is no wonder nobody is drawn to the Lord whom we claim to serve. Personally, if I thought being a Christian would make me as wretched as it seems to have made some that I have known, I would flee it as a pestilence.

But a Christian that is joyful is winsome. I think one secret of the rapid spread of Christianity over that stale and stuffy world of the long ago was its joyousness. When one of our best-known missionaries was speaking at a great banquet in South America, the presiding officer said to the speaker when the address was over: "I am an atheist. I do not accept your gospel, but I hope you are going to continue to preach it. You have a song in your heart, and we are very short on music." That is true of many all round the world. Joy is a sweet perfume that draws people as genuinely as the fragrance of the honeysuckle draws the bees in springtime. The joy of the Lord is your strength for winning others.

3. Then joy is at once our privilege and duty because such is the will of God for us. If you will turn through your Bible, it will astonish you how constantly it calls upon us to rejoice. "Be glad in the Lord and rejoice, ye righteous: and shout for joy, all ye that are upright in heart." "Rejoice in the Lord alway, and again I say, Rejoice." "These things have I spoken unto you, that my joy might remain in you, and that your joy might be full." Finally, as Jesus prays his last prayer with his friends at the end of the journey, one of his petitions is this—"That the joy that is mine may be theirs." God wills our joy because he knows that for us to be gloomy is to dishonor him as our Father. Above all else, he wills our joy because he loves us. We as fathers and mothers desire the happiness of our children. Therefore, it ought not to be hard for us to believe that God, our Father, desires the happiness of his children. Every man, therefore, ought to be joyful because it is only thus that we can be our best, that we can win others, that we can please God.

III

Now assuming that you have gone with me thus far, then what? Since everybody desires to be joyful, since everybody can be joyful, since everybody ought to be joyful for his own sake, for the sake of others, for the sake of his Lord, what are we to do about it? How can we find this joy? In other words, what sure word can I speak to you that are in life's green spring, as well as to you who are older grown, that will set your feet on the road to happiness? How can we have a good time?

Now there are certain roads that are quite popular that we must refuse to travel because they will not bring us to our desired goal. There are those, for instance, who believe that the way to have a good time is to attain a certain set of circumstances. These are not finding life very joyous now, but they are hoping to find it so when they attain a different set of circumstances. They are going to be joyful when we get into an ideal situation. But the first trouble with this is that there is no ideal situation. The second is, even if there were an ideal situation, you and I would likely fail to attain it. In the third place, even if we won it, it would likely cease to be ideal because we would soon mess it up. We are not going to live joyfully by getting into a perfect situation.

This is the case for the very simple reason that a good time is not a creature of circumstances. Whether we are joyous or not depends vastly more on what we are on the inside than anything that is on the outside. Of course, fortunate circumstances may add to our joy, but these can never be the source of a joy that abides. If a good time were a child of circumstances, then it would be easy to distinguish the joyful from the joyless. All we would have to do would be to find the healthful, the strong, the cultured, the successful, and put them on one side, and put the weak and the unfortunate and the sick and the failures on the other. Then we could say, "The former group is happy while the other is unhappy." But we know that this would not work at all. Some of the most miserable would be among the sons of good fortune while some of the most joyous would be among the sons of misfortune. If we ever attain joy, it is going to be an inside and not an outside job.

No more can we be joyous by sheer force of will. There are those who seem to believe that all one needs to do to have a good time is merely to square his jaw and say, "Go to now! I am going to fling away from all sadness and gloom and by my own bootstraps lift myself into the sunlight." Now I am not saying that we cannot help ourselves toward joy by an earnest effort, but this is not enough. There may be a bit of sanity in the old song, "Pack up your troubles in your old kit-bag, and smile, smile, smile," but smiles that are of real value do not begin on the outside and work in. They begin on the inside and work out. A smile set on the lips when there is a frown on the soul is a pathetically artificial thing with little of winsomeness about it. To have a good time we need more than a high resolve.

Then if we are going to capture the fortress of joy, we need more than a frontal attack. There are those in every age who give their days and nights to an effort to have a good time. I am not saying that they do not find any joy at all, that there is never a wisp of sunshine in their sky; but, generally speaking, they are dreadfully disappointed. "She that liveth in pleasure," said this man who urges us to joy, "is dead while she liveth." That is true. If you want to find the most weary and bored and fed-up people of any generation, go to those whose one purpose and aim in life is to have a good time. Others miss it, but these miss it most tragically.

How then, I repeat, can we live in our kind of world and have a good time? The first positive direction is this—keep peace with your conscience. You have a conscience. Of course, you can tamper with it until it ceases to be reliable. But even when its voice is not heard, it seldom ceases to speak. H. G. Wells tells of a man who was not so much a personality as a civil war. He was in constant conflict with himself. So long as an inner voice says "Don't," so long as an inner voice calls "Do this" and you disregard that voice, you will miss the real joy of living. "There is no peace, saith my God, to the wicked." Without peace there can be no real joy.

Not only is it necessary to keep peace with ourselves but with our brothers as well. I have known some poor haters and some rich haters, but I have never known a happy hater. To be at enmity with another is to carry about a bit of hell in your own heart.

Not only are we to be at peace with ourselves and with our brothers if we are to know joy, but we are to be at peace with God as well. "Woe unto him that striveth with his Maker!" But if we are at peace with God, if we have that peace that comes from the dedicating of our lives to him and to our brothers for his sake, then absolutely nothing can rob us of our joy. Whether we win or lose, whether we meet with success or failure in the eyes of the world, we shall surely find that which makes life rich and roomy and joyful.

Take, for instance, the man who wrote this text. He lived a hard life. There is no measuring the conflict and the suffering through which he passed. But more conspicuous than the harshness of his life was its richness and his joy. We find him at times without his friends. We find him without sufficient clothing to keep him warm. We find him without his beloved books. We find him without his freedom but never do we find him without his song. "Having nothing," he tells us with radiance looking out from his deep eyes, "having nothing, and yet possessing all things."

More conspicuous in his joy even than Paul was Paul's Master. Here is one whose life was one long crucifixion. It was one long climb up to Calvary. He was "a man of sorrows, and acquainted with grief." But in spite of that fact—yes, and because of it—his, I take it, was the gladdest heart that ever beat in a human bosom. His was the sunniest face that ever looked out on a troubled world. He was so joyous that he was an offense to the religious people of his day. They could give John the Baptist credit for being a religious man—he wore a camel's hair shirt and never went out to dinner. But this friendly man who was a great mixer with people, who was constantly calling his friends to be of good cheer, who was singing out of his own experience of the blessedness of the merciful and the meek—he could not be a good man! He was just a winebibber and a friend of publicans and sinners!

But if the joy of Jesus offended the strait-laced religionists of his day, it has cast a spell over countless millions who wanted to know his secret. Let us hear it from his own lips. "Take my yoke," he says, "for it is kindly." A strange word! The yoke that he wore was a yoke of perfect dedication to God. Thus being completely dedicated, he found life and joy in its fullness. So may we. About this I can be dogmatic. I have met dedicated men and women in all sorts of situations. Some worked in the limelight, and some worked in obscurity. Some were strong and vigorous, and some were being tortured on beds of pain. Some had plenty, and some were finding it hard to keep the wolf from the door. But there was one something common to all. They were joyous. Therefore, when Paul said, "Have a good time!" he was speaking to a universal longing, a universal privilege, and a universal obligation. If we meet the conditions of joy, we find it as naturally as night follows day, for it operates as the law of sowing and reaping. All dedicated lives are rich in joy.

XIV

I'D CLAIM MY OWN

"Ramoth in Gilead is ours, and we be still, and take it not."

I KINGS 22:3

A HAB AT HIS BEST WAS NOT MUCH OF A MAN. IT IS TRUE
that he had a heavy handicap. He was married to a
feminine cyclone named Jezebel. She would have endangered
the character and career of the strongest of men. Naturally
a man of the flabby fiber of Ahab had no chance at all. I
dare say that he never knew what sandals to put on any morning till he had asked Jezebel. But even Ahab cannot avoid
a certain amazed indignation at the folly of his own conduct as well as that of his brother king. "Ramoth in Gilead is
ours," he declares. Then he continues by saying in substance,
"But in spite of our ownership we are none the richer, because
we be still and take it not."

Now Ahab is by no means the only man who has been
guilty of this type of folly. This refusal to claim what rightfully is ours is a common tragedy. In Greek mythology

'Tantalus was condemned to the constant torture of a burning thirst and a gnawing hunger. Yet all the while that he was thus being tortured he stood in water up to his chin. But this water would vanish beyond his reach as he tried to drink it. All the while there were being dangled before his eyes the choicest fruits. But they would retreat beyond the reach of his hands when he tried to appropriate them. Thus he was persistently tortured by hunger and thirst that he could never satisfy.

But there is a worse hell even than his. That is to be tortured by the same hunger and thirst and yet to fail to win one drop of water or to taste one bite of food, not because such attainment is impossible, but because for some reason we refuse to claim what is offered. The man who misses life's prizes needlessly has the additional torture of having nobody to blame but himself. Tantalus could at least have the consciousness that he was doing his best. But the man who will not claim his own adds to the pain of his failure the further pain that his failure is his own fault.

I

What are some of the treasures that are ours at least in possibility?

1. There has perhaps come to all here present the privilege of being born into this land of freedom and opportunity. There are also open to almost all of us the privileges of physical well-being. We do not have to know the pangs of hunger such as are known by a large part of the world. While good health may not be in the reach of all of us, it is within reach of a far greater number than claim it. In addition, there are open to us educational opportunities. It is safe to say that

almost every young man or woman can have a college education if he or she really desires such a treasure.

2. But the most precious treasure that is open to us is the treasure of a Christlike character. Jesus was the supreme optimist. His optimism was born of his daring faith. To a superlative degree he believed in God. That was evident to his friends. That was evident also to his bitterest enemies. When he hung on the cross the worst that his murderers could say of him was, "He trusted in God." Jesus believed in the adequacy of God for his own needs and for the needs of the whole world with a faith that nothing could shake.

Believing thus profoundly in God, he also believed in man. He suffered at the hands of men as few have suffered. One of his inner circle swore that he did not know him. Another betrayed him with a kiss. All deserted him in his hour of supreme need. Yet he never lost faith in them. At the close of the day, in daring confidence, he firmly rolls the future of his Church upon their weak shoulders with the declaration that the gates of hell should not prevail against it. He faced the fact that though some men were lost, every one of them, even the worst, had in him the making of a saint. He was sure that every blundering and fluctuating Simon might be made into a rock of Christlike character. Being thus sure of the salvability of the individual, he also believed that the kingdoms of this world would one day become the Kingdom of God.

Believing thus that every man might become Christlike, he was also confident that every man might do a Christlike work. There were those then, as there are now, who made little contribution to this needy day. There were those then, as now, who not only failed to help but were positive hindrances. But he was sure that no man need be useless. He was sure that no man need be a hindrance. "He that believeth on me," he affirmed, "the works that I do shall he do also." Thus he is saying to us what he said to Abraham in the long ago, "I will bless thee, . . . and thou shalt be a blessing." Every one of us has the capacity for possessing a Christlike character and rendering a Christlike service.

3. Then, as we have possibilities as individuals, we have possibilities as a group. It would perhaps be too much to say that every marriage might be a success, but it is certainly true that far more might succeed than do. One marriage in every six goes upon the rocks. Many of the other five-sixths miss much of the romance and poetry of living. This is the case, not because a successful marriage was impossible. It is rather because, either through ignorance or selfishness or for some other reason, the contracting parties refused to claim their possibilities.

We have here a strong and helpful church. I love to believe that it is making a real contribution to you and to your city and to our whole state. But we have not yet achieved our best. There are many possibilities that we have not yet attained. It is the purpose of our Lord that we should be a glorious church without spot or wrinkle or any such thing. Wrinkles tell of the passing of youth and the coming of age. But the church that measures up to its possibilities is glorious in its youthfulness and, therefore, glorious in its daring. It is possessed of the spirit of adventure. Its sun always hangs in a morning sky. We need to possess our possession as a church.

Then God has made it possible for men to live in a brotherly world and to delight themselves with the abundance of peace.

When we think how bountiful this world is, we must realize how needless it is that so many thousands should suffer constant hunger. When we think how we are tearing our world apart at this moment, worse than wasting its material wealth and destroying that most priceless of all commodities, human life, we cannot fail to see how mad our conduct is! There is a bountiful and brotherly world for us in tomorrow if we are wise enough in the strength of God to claim it. How poor we are in every way in comparison with what we might possess if we would but claim the wealth that is really ours.

II

Why is it that we miss the priceless treasures that are offered so freely?

1. Some of us fail to claim what is ours because we think too meanly of ourselves. We allow ourselves to be handicapped by a sense of inferiority. In saying this we do not mean to indicate that humility is not a beautiful virtue. But to be truly humble is not to be in any sense wanting in self-respect. Jesus was a man who was perfect in humility. But in spite of that fact no man was ever girded by a nobler self-respect. To look with contempt upon oneself is to fail to claim what is rightfully ours.

2. There are others who fail because they think too meanly of the wealth that is potentially theirs. They look at the wares that are offered and see in them little of worth. That was the pathetic blunder of that fine animal, Esau. He had a birthright, the possibility of the religious leadership of his clan. But he despised that birthright. That means that he undervalued it. In his eyes it was worth less than a dish of beans. Therefore, he said to Jacob, "Behold, I am at the point to

die: and what profit shall this birthright do to me?" Then the author continues, "he did eat and drink, and rose up, and went his way." Thus undervaluing his birthright, life became for him a petty round of eating and drinking.

The Prodigal Son made a similar blunder. His opportunities were measureless. He had a home with the finest of fathers. But he felt that the life he was living was a cheap and mean affair in comparison with the life he could find if he were only on his own. His father could do much for him, but he could do far more for himself. Therefore he said, "Give me the portion of goods that falleth to me." Thus he traded wealth for want. Thus he gave up the companionship of his father for the companionship of a pigsty. He refused the best that his father offered because he rated those treasurers of little value.

3. Then some fail because they seek to claim their treasures on their own terms. The Elder Son was just as needy as his prodigal brother. He complained to his father that all his yesterdays had been pinched by poverty and slavery. "Lo these many years," he declared, "do I serve thee, neither transgressed I at any time thy commandment: and yet thou never gavest me a kid, that I might make merry with my friends." When, therefore, the feast was prepared for the returning prodigal, there was no man more hungry than he. Yet in spite of his hunger, he failed to go in because he demanded the feast on his own terms. He was eager to enjoy the feast as the reward of his own goodness rather than as a gift. But this was impossible. Therefore, the door to the banquet was shut in his face. We always miss our possibilities when we try to claim them on our own terms.

4. Finally, there are those who miss their possible treas-

ures because they lack the gallantry and the grit to claim them. Many a man rots down physically, mentally, and spiritually simply because he insists upon taking the easy way. The Ten Spies were all for entering the Land of Promise until they found that such an entrance would be costly. It might even involve bloodletting. Therefore, because they lacked the grit to possess what they believed was rightly theirs, they turned away saying, "We were in our own sight as grasshoppers."

One of the most charming characters in the New Testament is the Rich Young Ruler. He was clean, intelligent, and courageous. He was deeply in love with those values that are of supreme worth. One day, in his eagerness, he ran down the road to kneel at the feet of Jesus with this question: "What shall I do that I may inherit eternal life?" But when the Master answered his question by telling him that it would cost him the giving of his all, he went away. This he did, not because the article was of little worth, but because the price was greater than he was willing to pay.

Now it may be that I have not given your reason. Some, I say, fail because they think too meanly of themselves. Some fail because they think too meanly of the wares that God has to offer. Some fail through pride, some through lack of gallantry. Maybe you are failing because, though you do think well of yourself as a child of God, though you do appreciate the privileges offered you, yet you have never brought your actual claiming into the here and now. Bear in mind that, whatever may be your reason, if you fail to claim what is yours, the end is tragedy. In every gift there are two involved —the giver and the receiver. Even though the giver is God, if we refuse to receive, we defeat God's purpose for us and impoverish ourselves.

III

Before any gift, therefore, becomes ours, it must be appropriated.

1. That is true of material gifts. The best dinner in the world goes for nothing if we refuse to eat it. The finest farm is of no value unless we claim it by cultivating it. The sluggard had a fertile farm, but it did not save him from want. "I went by the field of the slothful, . . . and, lo, it was all grown over with thorns, and nettles had covered the face thereof, and the stone wall thereof was broken down." The field was his, but it was of no value because he was too lazy to possess it.

The same is often true of money. Some years ago I assisted in a meeting in Waco, Texas. There was a bedridden invalid near by, to whom the minister's wife would send a tray of food every so often. This poor invalid would nibble at that food sparingly to make it last as long as possible. At last she died. Her physician said that she died very largely of starvation. But when the neighbors went into that squalid little room to prepare the remains for burial, they found hidden in various places twenty thousand dollars in cash. She had wealth, but she did not know how to appropriate it. Thus it was of no more value to her than if it had been so much sawdust.

Do you remember *The Will* by James Barrie? One day a lovely young couple came into the gloomy office of a London solicitor for the husband to make a will. While the devoted wife realized the wisdom of her husband's making this will, the mere suggestion of his death that such a procedure implied moved her to tears. Since the young husband was just getting started in business, he naturally did not have much to leave. But in spite of this fact his wife insisted that he leave a small legacy to each of his two old maiden aunts—they were so dear and so needy! All in all, the whole interview was so delightful that when they were gone the old lawyer felt as if he had been having a stroll in a flower garden.

Ten years passed. The couple were again in the lawyer's office. This time the wife was present, but not because she had been invited. She had come, according to her own statement, just to see that her husband did not do anything foolish. During those ten years they had prospered beyond their hopes. Therefore, the husband had much more to bequeath. But the wife would not allow him to will a penny to his two old maiden aunts. They ought to have looked out for themselves and saved their money as she had done!

Ten more years pass, and the husband is again in the lawyer's office—this time alone. He has now grown very rich. Once more he has come to make his will. For a moment he glares fiercely at the old attorney and then blurts out, "My wife is dead. My daughter has run away with the chauffeur. My son is a rotter." Then he tossed a piece of paper on the desk saying, "There, take that. It has the names of the men with whom I have fought most fiercely for gold. Leave all my money to them with my respectful curses." He had money, but he did not in reality possess it.

2. The same is true in the realm of literature and art. Some years ago I was in the home of a wealthy man who led a busy life and a not unprofitable one. We were seated in his beautiful library, whose walls were lined with books. When

he had excused himself to be gone for a few moments, I got up to see what his taste was in reading. I found that the first volume I took from the shelf did not have the leaves cut. Then I tried another and another and another. The choicest books were there, books such as Milton describes as "the precious lifeblood of a master spirit embalmed and treasured up on purpose to a life beyond life." Yet had every book been blank, they would have been worth as much to him as those priceless volumes. Even the Word of God counts for nothing if we let it alone.

3. The same is true of the treasures we have in Jesus Christ. Though he says, "Son, thou art ever with me, and all that I have is thine," we may go through life as poverty-stricken as did this Elder Son to whom these words were spoken. Perhaps the greatest heartache of our Heavenly Father today is that he desires to do so much for us and we claim so little. How the Master yearned to give the beloved city of his fathers his best, but that city refused to claim it. "How oft would I . . . but ye would not." To the city, to the individual, to many of us today, he still has to utter that word, drenched with tragedy and soaked with tears: "Ye will not come to me, that ye might have life."

According to Paul, our treasure is all that God has. "All things are yours." Possibly we had better look into God's roomy hand and see if there is not something there that is worth our taking. He offers a new and better self. He offers his friendship and fellowship. "Thou art ever with me." He offers, I repeat, his very all. There is nothing that he has that is too good for you and me. But bear in mind that all that is necessary in order for us to miss this treasure is simply to let it alone. "How shall we escape, if we neglect?" There is no escape. If the best ever becomes ours, we must claim it.

That is a fascinating story in the second book of Kings. The city of Samaria is undergoing the horrors of a siege. Starvation is stalking every street. Four lepers hold a committee meeting in the gate of the city. One of them, a very wise man, asks this sanest of questions, "Why sit we here until we die?" First, he decided upon action. The next question was, what action? "If we go into the city," he continues, "we shall die." So that was ruled out. "Since it is death to sit still and death to go into the city, let us take the only chance that is left. It looks poor enough, but at least it does not make death a certainty. Therefore, let us fall unto the hosts of the Syrians." What was the result? When they reached this camp they found that the enemy had fled and that a feast was spread for them beyond their wildest dreams. But how did it become theirs? It became theirs not merely by their wishing but by their actually claiming. God's best is ours, but we can never experience that best unless in the here and now we claim it and make it our very own.

XV

I'D MAKE FOLKS TREAT ME RIGHT

"All things whatsoever ye would that men should do to you, do ye even so to them."

MATTHEW 7:12

HERE IS A DIRECTION FOR THE MANAGING OF OUR HUMAN relationships that is so excellent that men have given to it the name of the "Golden Rule." Of course, this name is not altogether fortunate. This great word of the Master is not a rule but a principle. A rule has a flavor of the arbitrary about it. A rule may be timely, but it is seldom timeless. But a principle is true in any place and in any age. This word of the Master is, therefore, just as fresh at this moment as it was when he uttered it, now nearly two thousand years ago. It tells us how we can get any response from our fellows that we desire.

I have a friend who was converted and called to the ministry after he had been for some years a law-enforcement officer. One day after he had become pastor of a prominent church in a certain Texas city, he chanced to park his car in front of a saloon. Now it so happened that this saloon was owned and operated by a man who was a notorious killer. When he discovered that the minister's car was parked before his door, he ordered him to remove it. "I own this saloon," he said, "and I will not have your car parked in front of it." But the minister, knowing the law, replied, "The fact that you own this saloon does not mean that you own the street." "Be that as it may," the saloon keeper replied, "you will move the car." Then the minister gave the bully his entire attention. "My friend," he said, "you can get anything out of me you want from a match to the Rocky Mountains. The car stays right where it is." And there it stayed.

Now what this minister was saying in his rude and positive way is generally true. We can get from our fellows, within certain limits, whatever response we desire. Of course, Jesus did not mean that this principle worked with mathematical exactness in every instance. He himself lived these great words before he ever uttered them. Always he put himself in the other man's place. Yet he did not elicit in every instance the response that he desired. Though he was the friendliest of men, he made bitter enemies. Though he truly loved all men, he died on a cross. Yet generally speaking, I repeat, this is abidingly true—we can get any response from others that we desire.

Here, then, is a word for all of us. It is a word especially fitting for those of us who feel that we are being cheated. There are a great many people who feel a grudge against life. They feel that their fellows have robbed them by their neglect. Often they are full of resentment. I used to know a young woman who collected grudges and slights and insults just as some collect stamps or old coins or antiques. She seldom came home from the office without having a new specimen to display. But her sad plight was not so much her misfortune as it was her own fault. Here is the way to get from others what you want: "All things whatsoever ye would that men should do to you, do ye even so to them."

I

What, then, assuming that we are normal men and women, do we desire from our fellows?

Please do not begin by saying, "I desire nothing at all. It doesn't matter to me in the least what folks think about me." If you make a declaration of that kind, the chances are overwhelmingly great that you are not telling the truth. In fact, generally speaking, the more loudly we protest our indifference to the good opinion of others, the more intense is our desire for that good opinion. It is very likely that we are protesting our indifference because we have been wounded. But if it so happens that we are telling the truth, our case is worse still. To be entirely indifferent as to what others think of us is to be self-centered and egotistical, almost beyond the human. Therefore, if we are normal we care. What do we desire from our fellows?

1. We desire that our fellows like us, that they like us enough to take a genuine interest in us. We hate being neglected and passed by. It gives us a sinking of the heart to have to say, "No man cares for my soul." It always warms our hearts to know that there are some who care enough for us to rejoice in our victories and to sorrow in our defeats and failures.

Not only do we desire that people take an interest in us, but we are eager for this interest to be based on what we are in ourselves. We do not wish to be valued mainly as a means, but as an end. The other day a gentleman greeted you with such warmth and enthusiasm that it refreshed you like a breeze from the sea. He proceeded to inquire about your health, about all your kinfolks, even your in-laws. Then just as you were blossoming into newness of life under the breath of this springtime, he produced a book that he was selling or he told you that he was eager for your support in the forthcoming election. That left you a bit cold. We desire that folks be interested in us for ourselves.

2. Then, we desire that our fellows look for the best in us instead of for the worst. We do not desire that our friends be faultfinders. We are conscious of the fact that if our fellows seek for the worst in us they will find it. This they will do regardless of how nearly perfect we may be. In fact, the one perfect man that this world has ever known was not exempt. There were those who sought for the worst in Jesus and succeeded so well in finding it that, to them at least, he had no "form nor comeliness; and there is no beauty that we should desire him." On the contrary, he was a mere gluttonous man and a friend of publicans and sinners.

Not only do our fellows who look for the worst in us find it, but they generally miss all that is good. The faultfinder so fixes his attention on the fault that he usually fails to see anything else. That is true in the reading of a book, the eating of a dinner, or the hearing of a sermon. Not long ago a layman was berating his pastor for preaching a certain sermon. When he told me his grievance, it added up to this—while the Scripture lesson was a gem, and while he agreed with ninety-nine per cent of what his minister said, there was one per cent to which he objected. Therefore, he threw away the ninety-nine per cent with which he agreed and carried away the one per cent that offended him. How silly! Even a cow, given a bundle of luscious hay with one briar in it, will eat the hay and leave the briar. But this man ate nothing but the briar! To look for the worst is to find the worst and nothing more. Naturally, therefore, we yearn for our fellows to judge us kindly and to look for the best in us. Looking for that, they will find it.

3. Finally, if we are normal, we want the appreciation of our fellows. We are eager that they appreciate us both for what we are and for what we do. Not only so, but we are eager for them to express their appreciation. Of course, there are times when we must be brave enough and strong enough to get on without it. There are times when we must carry on though nobody applauds and nobody approves. But while we must do this, there is no denying the fact that our work would be easier and our hearts would be lighter if our fellows would tell us of their appreciation.

To confess our love of appreciation is not merely to acknowledge that we are vain and childish. To make such a confession is to confess our kinship with our Lord himself. One day when he had cured ten lepers, only one came back to express his appreciation. "Were there not ten cleansed?" he asked, "but where are the nine?" These nine that failed to come brought him genuine grief. The one who did come made his heart sing. God himself loves our appreciation. Therefore, he urges through his prophet, "Let the redeemed of the Lord say so."

II

How, then, are we to win from our fellows the responses and reactions that we so deeply desire?

168

Let me begin by pointing out a few methods that we often try that fail to work. For instance, we cannot win the desired responses from our fellows by ignoring them. Yet that is the only method that some of us ever employ. We complain that we went to a certain church and nobody spoke to us. What we really mean is that we went to a church where there were hundreds of friendly people, but we refused to speak to a single one. In a recent issue of the *Saturday Evening Post* there is a story of a certain chap who went to a church in New York and sat through the entire service with his hat on. At the close of the service an usher said to that hat-wearer, "How come?"

"Well," he replied, "I have been coming to this church for twenty-six years. This morning I bet my wife that I could make one of you ushers speak to me."

By wearing the hat he won the bet. But he could have won it in a far better way. He could have won it by walking bravely up to that forbidding usher and holding out his hand and saying, "Smith is my name." But if you stand aloof and wait for another to make all the advances, you will likely be disappointed.

No more can we get from our fellows what we desire by meeting their seeming slights with a greater slight. "I met him," we say, "and he looked right through me, or he looked right over the top of my head." So what? "I treated him the same way. I showed him that I could be just as indifferent as he could." But indifference and resentment do not beget friendship. They beget indifference and resentment.

If we cannot win others by neglect and indifference, we certainly cannot do so by compulsion and violence. A good man whom I knew well said to his neighbor, as they were preparing to arbitrate a certain matter in dispute, "I am going to respect your feelings in this business, and you have got to respect mine." That was a bad start. If you were to put a gun in my face and say, "Love me, or I am going to blow your brains out!" I would fall in love then and there. But the chances are that when the artillery was removed, my love would wax cold.

Then we are not likely to be highly successful in getting the responses from others that we desire if we make these responses our goal. We are far more likely to arrive by the indirect road than by the direct. Neither can we compel the responses from others that we desire by being merely clever and highly successful. Cleverness and success often give us a good start, but these are not enough. Macbeth was a success. He won a crown. But he also won

> "Curses, not loud but deep, mouth-honor breath,
> Which the poor heart would feign deny, and dare not."

A few years ago a young man made a solo flight across the Atlantic. By so doing he won universal acclaim. His achievement was regarded as about the greatest of human history. Personally, I think it was overrated. But be that as it may, it did give this young man a place in the esteem of his people that no other man of his age has ever achieved. But he received this attention without any mark of appreciation. In fact, he seems often to have met efforts to do him honor with bored contempt. What is the result? From being the most honored man of his day, he has come, whether right or wrong, to hold a very small place in the honor and esteem of his people. His changed position means simply that he is getting what he has given. How, then, can we win what we desire?

1. If we desire the interest of our fellows, we must be interested in them. If we long for them to like us, the first big step is to like them. This will win when everything else fails. A man came to see me some years ago about whom I had heard much, and that much was not complimentary. I confess that I had a genuine and deep-seated prejudice against him. But he treated me in such a kindly fashion that when he left I said to myself, "I believe that fellow likes me." So what? I began then and there to like him. I could not help it.

When Will Rogers met his tragic death a few years ago, I think he was lamented by more people around the world than any other man in human history. Why was this the case? It was not true merely because he made the world laugh. That was a help. He laughed at and with all the prominent men of his day. But his laughter was never jarring. It was always gentle and kindly. Why, then, did millions feel that they had lost a friend? We find the answer in the words of Will Rogers himself. He said, "I never saw a man that I did not like." The surest way to have a friend is to be one.

2. We are eager for others to judge us kindly. This being the case, we should judge them kindly. This is what Jesus said, not only in this that we call the Golden Rule. He said the same in the opening verses of this chapter: "Judge not, that ye be not judged. For with what judgment ye judge, ye shall be judged: and with what measure ye mete, it shall be measured to you again." That may not always work out with mathematical accuracy, but, generally speaking, we are measured by our own yardsticks, we are weighed upon our own scales. If you assist a friend in picking your neighbor to pieces, the chances are that that neighbor will assist his friend in picking you to pieces. This is the case simply because our

critical attitude indicates a cold and loveless heart, and such a heart in us begets the same in others.

3. Then this word to you who are hungry for appreciation: Some of you are feeling that nobody cares whether you sink or swim, whether you live or die. "Nobody," you complain, "ever appreciates me. Nobody ever seems to be thankful." But examine yourself and see if you really appreciate anybody. Express your gratitude to your friend, and that friend will become grateful to you. He will become grateful for your gratitude if for nothing else.

III

Not only is this principle true in our relationship with each other, but it is true in a profound sense in our relationship to God. Our response to him conditions his response to us. There is a shocking word in the Old Testament that reads like this: "With the merciful thou wilt shew thyself merciful, and with the upright man thou wilt shew thyself upright. With the pure thou wilt shew thyself pure: and with the froward thou wilt shew thyself unsavoury." In other words it would seem that the prophet is claiming that God acts toward us as we act toward him. It would even seem that he is claiming that the Eternal God is possessed of our human frailties and weaknesses and wickednesses. It would seem as if he were claiming that God only loves us when we love him.

Of course, this is not what the author means. He knows that God loves all of us with an everlasting love regardless of our response to that love. But what he does mean is this—that God in the nature of things cannot act toward us as he longs to act except as we take a right attitude toward him.

God can no more give me what I refuse to take than the sunrise can illuminate my face if I turn my back to the sun. What we receive from God depends on our response to him.

When the Prodigal came home and the feast was spread, the Elder Son in angry resentment refused to share that feast. When his father went out to reason with him, the son made an assertion that he intended as a biting and cruel criticism of his father. It was this: "Lo, these many years do I serve thee, neither transgressed I at any time thy commandments: and yet thou never gavest me a kid, that I might make merry with my friends." What a shocking assertion to make about a good father! Yet, strange as it may seem, the father doesn't deny a word of it. His son has led the starved life of a slave in spite of his sonship. This the father cannot deny.

But why was this the case? It was not the fault of the father, but the fault of the son. This boy, in spite of his sonship, had insisted on treating his father as a slaveowner rather than as a father. Such an attitude had made it impossible for the father to do what he longed to do. Even while this son was living as a slave, this was his privilege: "Son, thou art ever with me and all that I have is thine."

Refusing thus to take the place of a son, he also refused to take the place of a brother. Therefore, when the Prodigal came home and a feast was spread and joy was unconfined, the Elder Son had no share in that joy. He rather became angry and embittered. Instead of giving his brother a brother's welcome, he did his best to drive him back into the old life. He did his best to tear open the old wounds that were just beginning to heal. "But as soon as this thy son was come," he says bitterly, "which hath devoured thy living with harlots." That even went beyond the record. He did not know this to be the case. Thus, refusing to act as a son and as a brother, he shut the door to the feast of the fullness of life in his own face.

We can readily see now why Jesus put such emphasis upon this golden word. "This," he declares, "is the law and the prophets." This sums up the whole teaching of the word of God. It is the very epitome of the gospel. To obey it is to receive the best from God and the best from man. Rightness with God and rightness with man must ever go hand in hand. "Thou shalt love the Lord, thy God, with all thy heart . . . and thou shalt love thy neighbor as thyself." These two cannot be separated. Some begin by loving God and pass on to the love of man as God's child. Others begin by loving man and pass on to the love of God as man's Father. Where we begin is not significant. It is the high goal that counts.

Suppose, then, we begin here and now to take Jesus seriously. We are all conscious, I dare say, that we do not love our fellows as we ought, that we are not always as interested, as kindly in our judgments, as appreciative as we might be. But in spite of that let us begin prayerfully to put into practice this great word in the here and now. As we practice it, we shall come more and more to receive from others the love we give. Thus we shall find it increasingly easy to give what we desire. Not only so, but as we thus obey we shall come increasingly to spiritual certainty. Increasingly, we shall hear the voice of our Master saying to us, "Inasmuch as ye have done it unto one of the least of these my brethren, ye have done it unto me." If, therefore, you are eager to receive God's best and man's best, I commend to you this matchless word, "All things whatsoever ye would that men should do to you, do ye even so to them."

XVI

I'D GROW UP

"I put away childish things."

I CORINTHIANS 13:11

PAUL IS HERE MAKING A TREMENDOUS ASSERTION. HE does not claim that he has put away the childlike. To do that would not be triumph but tragedy. He claims that he has put away the childish. As he has come to physical maturity, so he has reached some degree of mental and spiritual maturity. A little baby is a beautiful creature that excites our love and expectation. The coming of a seven-pound baby into a home is something to make the heart sing. But suppose the baby, instead of weighing seven pounds, should weigh 150. That would not make for laughter, but for tears. In fact, the infancy of the grownup is one of life's crowning tragedies.

I

"I put away childish things." What are these childish things? There are certain characteristics that mark us as childish regardless of our age.

1. Little children are much given to tears. We expect them to weep more or less, therefore their wails do not greatly upset us. Not only do babies weep, but they weep over trifles as well as over things that really matter. It does not take a deadly wound to make them cry out. A slight pin scratch will serve just as well. They howl at a touch of colic, or if dinner is a few minutes late. There is nothing too small to upset their little world and cause them to yell at the top of their lungs.

Not only are babies easily moved to tears, but their crying is always over some personal calamity. What those about them may be suffering matters nothing. The slightest pain upsets them far more than an earthquake in a neighboring city or even a world war. They weep easily but always for themselves. Never do they have a tear for the woes and wants of others.

2. A second characteristic of the infant is his love of attention. He must have the center of the stage. That is one reason he cries. When he grows a bit older, that is the reason he displays his sore toe. That is the reason, when he grows older still, that he tells you how badly life has treated him, that he gives you a blow-by-blow description of what his nerves are doing, that he informs you of his operation and ends by fervently hoping that you will never have to suffer as he has suffered.

Sometimes his love of attention takes another direction. He is willing to work, but only when he is in the lead. He is willing to play, but only when he chooses the game. If he is voted down, he refuses to be a good democrat. Instead, he sulks in his tent and goes no more to battle. He washes his hands of the whole business, declaring emphatically, "My way is right. I am always right, and if you don't do my way then I am through."

There is no measuring the harm that such big babies work in the ordinary business of living. They can be terribly in the way in the church. Often they can wreck a home. Some time ago I married a young couple, one of whom had not grown up. When the wife did something that displeased this big baby, instead of talking it over with her, he puffed up and pouted and had her guessing at what was wrong. Sometimes it is the other way round. The husband goes to work and forgets to kiss his wife good-by, or he fails to remember an anniversary. Then when he comes home at night, she looks like a chronic pain. When he asks an explanation, she refuses to give it. Such people are too childish to make a success out of the big adventure of marriage.

Then often we show our childishness by demanding appreciation. Of course, everybody loves appreciation. It is far harder to carry on when nobody approves. But to fail to do so is not a mark of maturity but of the opposite. The baby produces a bit of a sensation when he takes his first step. Everybody gathers about to applaud. But if the child expects that applause to continue throughout life, he is likely to be disappointed. If he reaches the place where he refuses to walk without it, then it means he has never grown up. The childish must have attention. They like the center of the stage. Some even commit crimes just to see their names in the paper.

3. A third mark of childishness is the taking of life's blessings as a matter of course. Accepting them as their deserts, babies naturally have no sense of gratitude. You may trot a colicky baby on your knees for half the night, but

he will never show the slightest appreciation. When did ever a baby look into a tired mother's eyes and say, "Thank you"? We can take such ingratitude from little babies, but from big ones it is far harder to bear. There are few uglier signs of perpetual infancy than never to learn to say either to God or man, "I thank you."

4. A fourth mark of infancy is to have no sense of obligation. Whenever a child begins to want to give back something for what he has received, we are encouraged. That means that he is growing. But there are those in whom a sense of obligation never develops. They are always thinking in terms of what the world owes them, never in terms of what they owe the world. Some time ago I saw a frail-looking mother walking down the street with an unusually husky youngster. This vigorous lad walked along beside her for a little while. Then he decided that he would ride. So he began to demand that his mother carry him. She sought to reason with him, tried to tell him how weary she was. But his only answer was to run in front of her, seize her around the knees, and stop her in her tracks. Then she took the giant into her arms, and I did not know which one needed the woodshed the more. Such clamoring to be carried is bad even in a lad of three, but in one of forty it is utterly hideous.

5. Finally, childish folks are selfish. All small children are self-centered. The fact that they wail over their own petty disappointments and over theirs only, their demand for attention, their lack of a sense of gratitude and of obligation, all these are but the streams that flow from the fountain of self-centeredness. Selfishness is never winsome. Old people may be very ugly or they may be very beautiful. When

they are ugly, their crowning ugliness, generally speaking, is born of the fact that they have become childish.

Years ago I was invited to dine in a certain home of whose tragedy I was entirely ignorant. Therefore, you can imagine something of my amazement, upon my arrival at that home, when I saw a man fully six feet in height playing about on the lawn clad in a checked apron of the style that he wore when he was two or three years of age. More than a score of years before a baby had gladdened that home. But the sunshine that he had brought had now changed into the blackest of shadows. This was the case because, though he had grown in body, he had never grown in mind and heart. His was the tragedy of perpetual infancy. To refuse to put away childish things is to become a grief to both God and man.

II

Not only did Paul put away childish things, but for his immaturity he substituted maturity. What are some of the marks of maturity? What is there about Paul that indicates that he has really become a man?

1. The fact that Paul has grown up does not mean that he has put away tears altogether. He still weeps, but he no longer weeps over petty trifles. Nor are his tears shed simply for troubles personal to himself. He can, of course, still weep over his own sorrows. Our Lord does not call upon us to hate ourselves and to love our neighbors. He calls upon us to love our neighbors as we love ourselves. But while Paul still weeps, his tears are now almost wholly for others. "Ye know," he writes, "from the first day that I came into Asia, after what manner I have been with you at all seasons,

serving the Lord with all humility of mind, and with many tears, and temptations, which befell me by the lying in wait of the Jews." His tears are like the tears of his Master. They are born of his heartache for others. They indicate that self has died under the stroke of the Cross, and that he has truly learned to rejoice with those that do rejoice and to weep with those that weep.

2. Paul can now carry on when nobody applauds. This does not mean that he does not care for the approval of his fellows. Every sensitive soul longs for such approval. But it does mean that if this approval is withheld, he does not give over and quit. "I will very gladly," he writes, "spend and be spent for you, though the more abundantly I love you the less I be loved." He has not only reached the place where he can carry on when nobody applauds, but even when folks ignore or disapprove, or become positively antagonistic. That is a mark of maturity.

3. The fact that Paul has grown up is further indicated by his deep sense of gratitude. In truth, that is one of his most beautiful characteristics. As we follow his eventful life, we find him in all sorts of trying and perplexing situations. Sometimes he is at the whipping post, sometimes in personal danger, sometimes he is putting through difficult tasks with no human backing. Again we find him in prison without his beloved books and without even a coat to keep him warm. But we never find him without his song of gratitude. "In everything," he writes, "give thanks." That has become the habit of his life. Blessed is the man who has so attained. I know no surer mark of maturity than a constant gratitude that grows out of our realization that we have nothing that we have not received either from God or from our fellows.

4. Finally, Paul indicates that he has become of age by his deep sense of obligation. "I am debtor," he writes. Having received so much and so persistently, he feels that he is under vast obligations to serve. Such a sense of obligation is always a mark of maturity. To be utterly lacking in it is always to remain an infant.

When the ancient Greeks sought to teach this lesson, they told how, when Achilles was born, his mother consulted the oracle to inquire as to the future of her son. That oracle told her that Achilles would either live a short life of battle and of victory or a long life of inglorious ease. Being a mother, and a mistaken mother at that, she chose the latter course. Therefore, she dressed him like a girl and hid him on an island where nobody lived but girls. He looked like a girl, played like a girl, and everybody thought he was a girl.

Then came the war against Troy. When the Greeks consulted the oracle as to how they might win, they were told that they could never win without Achilles. But nobody knew where Achilles was. Therefore, Ulysses set out to find him. At last he came to the island where nobody lived but girls. He disguised himself as a peddler. He filled his pack with the trinkets and toys that girls love, but underneath he put a sword and a suit of shining armor. When he reached the island and displayed his wares, the girls bought eagerly. But one girl looked on with indifference, even contempt. Then Ulysses displayed the sword and the armor. At once the indifferent girl became all eargerness. She seized the sword and wielded it. She fitted on the armor. "Here," cried Ulysses, "is our hero!" He recognized him because he chose weapons instead of toys. In thus choosing he showed a sense of obligation.

But to have no sense of oughtness is always to remain a child. Children love to play. That is all to the good. For them playing is an end in itself. As we grow older, we ought still to play. We cannot render our best service without it. But with grownups playing must be a means to an end rather than an end in itself. There are many names by which I should not like to be called. There are few that I would hate more than this—"Playboy." To have come and grown and gone and never to have felt the hand of compulsion laid upon me, never to have said with my Master, "I must!"— that is about as damning a sin as one can commit.

III

Now how did Paul become a man? He did not do so by pulling up all the childish weeds in the garden of his soul one by one. No more did he change from moral and spiritual infancy into maturity in an instant. There was no magic about his coming to manhood. How, I repeat, did it come about? It was not instantaneous, it was a process. Paul became a man by growing.

Growth is an amazing miracle. No wonder Thomas Carlyle, holding a baby in his arms, looked at it with eyes of wonder. "Just to think," he said, "that Shakespeare was once like this!" And so he was! So was Hitler! So was Mussolini! So was Paul! So even was Jesus! When Luke undertakes to tell us how Jesus became the perfect Man that he was, he tells us that it was because he grew in the right direction. "Jesus increased in wisdom and stature, and in favor with God and man."

Seeing that Paul became mature by growth, how did he grow? How may you and I grow? It may help us to realize that growth under proper conditions is the most natural thing in the world. We do not grow by merely spitting on our hands. We do not grow by saying, "Go to, now! I am going to cease to be small and become large." Growth is a law of life. We grow, not by trying, but by meeting the conditions of growth. Here, for instance, is a normal, healthful baby. How does that baby grow? Not by worrying about it. He grows naturally, spontaneously, unconsciously, as he meets certain conditions. What are those conditions?

1. He eats. In fact, he seems little more than an appetite. If he fails to eat, he not only fails to grow but he dies. As food is necessary for the baby, so it is for you and me if we are to reach the kind of Christian manhood that was experienced by Paul. Why do so many who unite with the Church fail to make any progress? Why are they so often no bigger at the end of the day than they were at the beginning? For mulitudes this is the answer : They fail to get the right kind of food. They make little or nothing of prayer. They seldom look into God's Word. Thus they do not give themselves a chance to feed on the Bread of Life. One might as well expect to become a strong athlete by feeding on wind as to become a mature Christian by feeding on a diet that has in it no food for either mind or heart.

Some years ago a small group of scientists got lost in the wilds of Australia. They ran out of food. In their extremity they found the root of a certain plant that was palatable. But, though they ate of this heartily, they died to a man. When their bodies were found and the contents of their stomachs tested, it was found that the root they had been eating was absolutely devoid of food value. Such is the case with the diet upon which many professing Christians are trying to feed themselves today. They are careful about vitamins for the body while the diet upon which they seek to feed their minds would not contain a vitamin to the carload.

2. A healthy baby grows not only by eating but by exercise. A good bit of his yelling is nature's way of developing his lungs. When he kicks and tries to swallow now his foot and now his fist, he is taking his daily dozen. He is giving himself a workout. As exercise is necessary for a growing baby, so it is for a growing Christian. The low state of health of many church people may be explained by the fact that they never take any exercise.

Let me speak this personal word to you who have come to question the reality of religion. Have you found in your Christian experience more of weight than of wings? Has God become as vague for you as a dream? Then go out today and take a little exercise by serving others. Jesus declared, "For the Son of man is come to seek and to save that which is lost." Set yourself for a single day on that same mission and see what happens. It is perfectly marvelous how doubt melts in the warmth of an effort to do some good in the world. Growth is sure and natural when we eat the right kind of food and take the right kind of exercise.

3. Finally, the baby, having eaten and taken his daily dozen, goes to sleep. If we are to grow, we need not only food and exercise but rest as well. I am not now speaking mainly of rest for the body, though that is essential. Only this week I had a communication from an old school friend who has had to give up his work. He explained his breakdown in these words: "I have run past too many stop lights." Physical rest is good and essential. The man who works hard and fails to rest is sinning against God and his own body.

But the rest of which I am thinking now is that inward rest that Jesus promised when he walked among men. It is the rest that he promises now. Today, as in the long ago, he is saying to you and to me: "Come unto me, all ye that labor and are heavy laden, and I will give you rest. Take my yoke upon you, and learn of me; for I am meek and lowly in heart: and ye shall find rest unto your souls." Accept this invitation wholeheartedly, and you will know the gladness of growth. More and more you will experience one of the chief joys both of the life that now is and of that which is to come, the joy of growing. "Beloved, now are we the sons of God, and it doth not yet appear what we shall be: but we know that, when he shall appear, we shall be like him; for we shall see him as he is." Surely one of the richest privileges both of time and of eternity is the privilege of growing more and more into the likeness of our blessed Lord!

XVII

I'D TRY TO KEEP MY FOOTING

"I almost slipped, I nearly lost my footing."

PSALM 73:2 (MOFFATT)

O F ALL THE DEVOTIONAL BOOKS IN THE LITERATURE OF the world, this amazing hymnbook of the Jews is still the best known and the best loved. Though it came out of a long-gone past, though it was born in a civilization that was simple and primitive, yet it has managed to be at home in civilizations that have become increasingly complex. This book is as fresh today as the day it was written. This is the case because it comes out of experience. It speaks the language of the heart. Thus, it has something vital to say to us. This is the case because, as George Eliot reminds us, the heart of humanity is the same through the years, ever pulsating to the same great needs, the same great loves and longings.

This psalmist is seeking to share with us his own personal experience. He is telling us of a triumph that came very near ending in tragedy. From a certain mountain height he is looking back over his yesterdays. As he views the road along which he has traveled, he sees one bit where he had great difficulty. "Here," he declares, "I came very near slipping. My feet threatened to give way under me. But the threatened disaster was averted. Somehow by the good grace of God I won through."

I

Now this word is of vital interest to all of us.

1. It is interesting, in the first place, because there are some of you whose experiences have been close akin to that of this psalmist. As you look back across the years, there is perhaps some particular experience that stands out. There were desperate days that tried your soul. You, too, came very near losing your footing. But when the foul fiend Apollyon bestrode your path and "threatened to spill your soul" you took refuge underneath the everlasting arms and found God's grace sufficient. For this reason your struggle that was so trying yesterday is now one of your most precious memories.

Then there are others who will be interested in this story because they are now facing just such a conflict. Perhaps you are in the midst of it even now. Today you are being hard-pressed, today you walk in slippery places, today it seems an open question whether you will be able to keep your footing or not. Therefore, you are interested in this fighter of the long ago. Since he won through, you watch him with keen interest that you may learn his secret.

Perhaps another group will look on this scene with interest because it reminds them not of a triumph of yesterday but of a tragedy. This victorious fighter may remind you of a fight that you lost. Listening to his story you are reminded of a time when you did not almost lose your footing but lost it altogether. But though you fell, you did not then and there surrender. You tried again and again. You sought to brace yourself with Browning's great conviction that "we fall to rise, are baffled to fight better." But in spite of it all you failed, so that now your religious experience is little more than a memory.

We have all known men and women of this kind. Years ago I became deeply interested in a man whose one big fault was that he was a bondslave of drink. By and by he was converted. He became active in my church. He seemed to enjoy his religious life beyond the ordinary. But he secured a new position that threw him with the boon companions of his yesterday. He fell and made a new start, only to fall again. Years after I left the city I met him again. His once joyous face looked as dead as a parchment. "I have disgraced myself, my family, and my church," he said. "I will never try again." His feet had slipped so many times that he had completely lost heart and hope.

II

What was it that came so near upsetting this psalmist?

We are to bear in mind that the singer of this song was a deeply serious, a genuinely religious man. He did not, therefore, find the going slippery because he was careless and indifferent. What would knock my feet from under me might not trouble you at all. What would upset you might give me no difficulty. This psalmist found the going hard, however, for reasons that we can all understand. His experience has something to say to every man.

The beginning of his difficulty was that the facts of life

that he saw and experienced failed to check with his faith. What was his faith? Assuming that it was the same as that of the ordinary pious Jew, he believed that God was King. He affirmed, with other believers, "The Lord reigneth; let the people tremble." "The Lord reigneth; let the earth rejoice." The people were to tremble because the God who was reigning was a holy and almighty God who was "of purer eyes than to behold evil." The earth was to rejoice because the kingship of a holy God must make for righteousness upon the earth. One would naturally expect that, with a holy and omnipotent God upon the throne, this world would be governed as a world should be governed.

Because every pious Jew believed in God's kingship, he was convinced that the man who did right always came out first and best, while the man who did wrong always met with disaster. He was sure that a good man prospered in purse as well as in his soul. He was sure that a bad man always went to the wall financially and otherwise. That was the faith of Job's comforters. When they saw that Job was a great sufferer, they concluded at once that he was a great sinner. It simply could not be otherwise. "Who ever perished," they asked, "being innocent?" That was the faith of the disciples of Jesus when they asked, "Who did sin, this man or his parents, that he was born blind?"

This is a faith that is held by quite a few to this day. It dies hard. This is the case because there is so much of truth in it. Other things being equal, the good man stands a better chance to prosper financially and physically as well as spiritually than the man who is not good. Yet to go out with the complacent faith that the good always prosper as the world measures prosperity is to have your faith torn to bits just as was the case with this ancient psalmist. He saw that conviction flatly contradicted before his very eyes and in his own experience.

For instance, there were people all about him who ignored God, who were not the least religious, who had little or no respect for the rights of others; yet these seemed to be getting on famously. Perhaps one of them was a next-door neighbor. He knew how godless this man was, how thoroughly wicked. Every day he looked to see God strike him down, but the expected disaster failed to materialize. Instead, the man seemed in every way to prosper. His investments turned out well. His eyes fairly stood out with fatness. He had more than heart could wish.

Not only did the wicked neighbor prosper in purse, but he seemed also to have a good time. While he himself, the saint, was fretting, worrying, and stewing, this sinner seemed to be going joyously along his carefree way. Watching him thus so full of laughter, this psalmist concluded that the wicked were not in trouble as other men; neither were they plagued as others. He became convinced that though the saints might get more of heaven by and by, the sinners were certainly getting whatever heaven there might be in the here and now.

Not only was this wicked neighbor of his prosperous both in things and in laughter, but, having nobody to thank for his prosperity but himself, he was full of pride. He swaggered. The psalmist declared that he wore pride about his neck like an ornament. He wore his purple and fine linen with such a disgusting swagger that it was hard for the onlooker to keep from wishing that it were sackcloth. He lived in a palace with such selfish pomp that the beholder would have been glad to have seen that place turn into a pigsty.

Being proud, this godless neighbor was also violent. The psalmist declares that he wore violence as a garment. That was the natural outcome of his pride. If you are beneath me, if I am made out of finer material than you are, then there is no reason that I should respect your rights. Perhaps this saint had to watch his prosperous neighbor cheat and defraud the poor, then add insult to injury by boasting about it. "How doth God know?" he asks scornfully, "and is there knowledge in the most High?" What he is implying is that God does not count at all. Meantime God seemed to look on and do nothing.

Then, as a crowning and final offense, this wicked neighbor was not only prosperous, but by his prosperity he was winning the admiration of his fellows. "So people turn to follow them," Moffatt translates it, "and see no wrong in them." These thoughtless people never thought of asking how their prosperous neighbor had won his wealth. They were only impressed by the fact that he had won it. You can see that they are close akin to us. We are great success worshipers. Our hats are off to the man who gets on, generally speaking, regardless of the price he pays. We look with some respect to the man who had rather be right than president. But we shout for the man who gets to be president whether he is right or wrong. This man came very near being trapped by the prosperity of the wicked.

Not only did he find the prosperity of the wicked hard to bear, but he found the lack of prosperity on the part of the righteous even more upsetting. That was especially true because one of the righteous was none other than the psalmist himself. He was no doubt deeply religious. He had read his Bible, prayed, tithed, gone to church, tried to be just to his fellow man. But nothing enriching had come of it. Instead he complains, "All the day long have I been plagued and chastened every morning." As to the nature of his chastisement we cannot be sure. Perhaps the little business in which he invested his all went to the wall and left him with the wolf howling at his door. This was possibly followed by the loss of his health. In fact, life had come to mean for him just one calamity after another.

How, then, could he believe in a good God when the wicked prospered and the righteous failed? How could he keep up his faith when right was so constantly on the scaffold and wrong so persistently on the throne. It was hard for him to believe that he had not been duped. " 'Tis all in vain," he sobs, "I kept my heart from stain, kept my life clean!" Therefore he naturally asked himself: Why should I not use the worldling's methods and thus win his rewards? Why should not I, as my rich neighbor, "take the cash and let the credit go." This he was sorely tempted to do. Yet in spite of this temptation he managed to keep his feet. When the facts of life clashed with his faith, he found a finer faith that kept him going.

III

How did he do it? There are many helps that are available to us in our hours of crisis. But I am going to mention only the help that this psalmist found sufficient. Here he is standing firmly once more with a serenity in his heart that looks out through his eager eyes.

"How did you win?" I ask.

The answer is so simple as almost to provoke a smile.

"How did I win? I went into the sanctuary of God," is the shameless answer. How trite that sounds! Church attendance may be thoroughly stale and unprofitable. If we treat it as an end rather than a means, we are not likely to be greatly helped by it. Jesus tells of a certain gentleman who went to church—hard, cold, and full of pride. This man had a good eye on himself, a bad eye on his brother, and no eye on the Lord at all. Therefore when he prayed he only stood up to congratulate the Lord on having such a perfect servant as himself. Naturally his church attendance had done nothing for him but leave him a little more frostbitten and unbrotherly than he had been before.

But while church attendance may be a very trifling matter, it need not be so. According to Jesus there was another man, a publican, who attended the same service as did the Pharisee; but instead of being hardened he was transformed. It was not, therefore, any difference in the service that accounts for the different effects experienced by the Pharisee and the publican. It was the difference in the response made by the men themselves. One went to boast and the other went to worship.

Here is another man who found church attendance rewarding. He was a brilliant young aristocrat. He was a hero worshiper, but his hero was dead and his best dreams had died with him. In his desperation he entered, as did this psalmist, into the sanctuary. So what? "I saw the Lord sitting upon a throne, high and lifted up. . . . Then said I, Woe is me! for I am undone; because I am a man of unclean lips, and I dwell in the midst of a people of unclean lips: for mine eyes have seen the King, the Lord of hosts. Then flew one of the seraphims unto me, having a live coal in his hand, which he had taken with the tongs from off the altar: And he laid it upon my mouth, and said, Lo, this hath touched thy lips; and thine iniquity is taken away, and thy sin purged. Also I heard the voice of the Lord, saying, "Whom shall I send, and who will go for us? Then said I, Here am I; send me." Life for Isaiah took on a new departure that day because he attended church.

We need not be surprised, then, that when this sorely tried psalmist entered into the sanctuary of God, when he went as an earnest seeker after God, he did not go in vain. He came to a new awareness of God. He came to see life from God's viewpoint. Mounting through worship upon wings as eagles, he got a clearer view of our world. He came to estimate values somewhat as God estimates them. Seeing thus, he discovered that he was thoroughly mistaken both about his wicked neighbor and about himself.

1. He was mistaken about his neighbor. As a new understanding came to him, he realized that, though his neighbor was just as prosperous as he ever was, his prosperity was all on the outside of him. He saw that though he was rich in things, he was poor in soul. It was just when the rich fool was most conscious of his outside wealth that he became so keenly conscious of his inward poverty that he had to urge his starved soul to take a little nourishment. "Eat, drink, and be merry," he coaxed. He saw further that the man whose prosperity is all on the outside is not in reality prosperous at all. In spite of all his success, he was "consumed with terrors." With all his getting he had failed to find any real satisfaction.

This singer realized further that not only was this godless

man suffering from inward poverty in spite of his outward prosperity, but that even his outward prosperity was destined quickly to slip from his fingers. That is true of all wealth that consists of things. It fails to satisfy for the brief time that it is ours. Very quickly it is gone. The prosperous sinner spreads himself like a green bay tree; but, at a second look, not only his prosperity but he himself is gone. That is true of the least. It is true also of the greatest. Outward prosperity does not satisfy while it is ours. Even if it should, it is soon gone.

2. His second discovery was of his own vast wealth. He was unspeakably rich in God. "I am continually with thee:" he sings. "Thou hast holden me by my right hand." He came to realize that, for those who walked with God, hard times do not necessarily mean bad times. He was having a hard time when he went to church. No doubt he continued to have a hard time when the service was over. But he came to see that, instead of hard times being bad times, they often bring far greater wealth than good times.

Toward the end of his ministry Jesus spoke of certain coming events that seemed fraught with utter disaster. He foretold the destruction of the sacred city of Jerusalem. He showed how one dire calamity was going to stalk hard upon the heels of another. Then he ended with this amazing sentence. "When these things begin to come to pass, then look up, and lift up your heads; for your redemption draweth nigh." Deliverance often treads close upon the heels of tragedy for a very obvious reason. These tragic experiences, by destroying our self-sufficiency, make us willing to give God a chance.

It was along such a road that our psalmist traveled to

victory. He had been sorely tempted and perplexed. The prosperity of the wicked had upset him. The disaster that had dogged his own steps had upset him yet more. But when in his desperation he found God, he found also that outward circumstances were not vastly important. He went on suffering in many respects just as he had before. "My flesh and my heart faileth," he cries. But, having God, he found that he was possessed of all that life needed. "Whom have I in heaven but thee," he shouts, "and there is none upon earth that I desire beside thee." Finding God sufficient for all his needs in the here and now, he was sure that he would find him sufficient to the end of eternity. Braced by this high faith, his feet became like hind's feet. He possessed the sure-footedness of the deer as he walked to the end of his earthly pilgrimage. May such an experience be yours and mine!

XVIII

I'D USE MY HANDICAPS

"Before I was afflicted I went astray: but now have I kept thy word."

PSALM 119:67

HERE IS A MAN WHO IS TELLING US A BIT OF HIS EXPErience. This word is autobiographical. It comes up out of life. Coming thus out of life, it is of vital interest to you and me. This man once lived in our world. He has experienced something of our joys and sorrows. He has tasted the bitterness of affliction. Not only so, but he has used his affliction for his enrichment. Having thus won, he comes to share with us some of the rich knowledge that life has brought him. Therefore, he is well worth our attention.

I

The fact, however, that this singer has a worthful word to say to us does not mean that he has lived a flawless life. Though our present interest in him is due largely to the fact that he has now learned how to use his handicaps, such fine knowledge was not always his. In fact, there was a time when he did not even have the wisdom to use his advantages. He tells us frankly that before he was afflicted, before he knew the hampering grip of a handicap, he made a mess of his life. There was a time when he had used his fine, God-given powers, not in the service of God and man, but only to waste them either in selfishly decent or in riotous living.

His is a quite common experience. I am trying to preach to you on how to use your handicaps, but I do this in the realization that a sermon on how to use your advantages might be equally in order. It is exceedingly easy to take what is worthful into our hands and to use it in such a fashion as not only to make it worthless but to make it positively harmful. Many a man has changed his wealth into want, his capital into dire calamity.

Take material wealth, for instance. Money is power. It can give vast advantages. It can open doors that are often shut in the face of poverty. With money in their hands it need be said of no bright youths,

> "But Knowledge to their eyes her ample page
> Rich with the spoils of time did ne'er unroll;
> Chill Penury repressed their noble rage,
> And froze the genial current of the soul."

Yet plenty of money is more often a handicap than a help.

I read somewhere that years ago a boat, whose passenger list was made up largely of miners returning from the gold fields of California, went down in the middle of the Mississippi. When these miners saw that the vessel was doomed, most of them unbuckled their money belts, heavy with gold, and threw them upon the deck. They loved gold, yet they loved life more. But one miner, a strong swimmer, thought his comrades mad. Therefore, he eagerly picked up those heavy belts one by one and fastened them about this own body. Thus he became for the moment possessed of vast wealth. But when he sprang into the water, he sank to the bottom as if he himself had been made of gold. Thus, as often happens, he was wrecked by the very richness of his treasure.

A kindred tragedy threatens those who are gifted with physical strength and beauty. What a physical poem Lady Hamilton must have been! She must also have possessed some real personal charm along with it. Through that beauty and charm she climbed until she became the mistress of about the most famous admiral England ever had. But when we look with open eyes at the price she paid for her winnings, when we realize the pathetic end of her tragic career, we cannot but be convinced that she would have been far better off if she had been an ugly duckling rather than the physical poem that she was.

Some of you have perhaps read that recent book entitled *Good Night, Sweet Prince*. It is the story of a very unheroic man who was to the author a real hero. That John Barrymore was a man of immense charm and ability nobody can deny. I doubt that a greater Hamlet ever appeared on the American stage. He had such vast gifts that he could dash in a single night from obscurity into the limelight that plays about a star. What strength of mind and body he must have possessed! According to the author, it took 640 barrels of raw liquor to wreck that fine body and to blow out, in some measure, the brilliant light within that brain. Yet how little he accomplished! How few were enriched by him! I cannot but believe that life would have been richer for him if he had been mediocre both in body and mind. He did not know how to use his wealth.

Such had been the experience of this psalmist. "Before I was afflicted," he declares, "I went astray." Just how he went astray, we are not told. He may have gone in a quite decent and respectable fashion. He may merely have taken his gifts and used them all for himself. He may have been as decent as decency and respectable as respectability. Again, he may have had his fling. He may have sowed his wild oats. He may have gone into the far country and wasted his substance with riotous living. But whether decently or as a profligate, he had turned his back on God and gone astray. Thus had he failed to have the wisdom to use his advantages.

II

Then one day, like a bolt from the blue, something happened to him. He was overtaken by affliction. He came to be possessed of a handicap. His clear skies were overcast by scudding storm clouds. The daylight about him changed to darkness. The elasticity went out of his step. Perhaps the laughter went out of his eyes. As to the nature of his affliction, it is impossible to say. It may be that he lost his wealth and that the wolf of want began for the first time to howl at his door. It may be that he lost his health, so that pain now walked with fire-shod feet along every nerve of his tortured body. It may be that he lost his loved ones, so that there was now an emptiness where there was once a companionship and a desolation where there was once a home. But whatever the nature of his affliction, there came a blackout that made him one of the handicapped.

But in spite of the fact that we do not know just the nature of this man's handicap, of this we are sure—he knew the bitterness of affliction. Being thus handicapped, we know also that he is a member of a very large company. Life has not been all tragedy for any of us, thank God! But in spite of that fact, few of us have found it a bed of roses. If I could sit down by any one of you and listen to your story, it would probably be a story of handicaps, of hindrances, of difficulties that you would gladly have avoided. There may be exceptions to this rule, but I doubt that there is a single person present who is one hundred per cent fit. Therefore, this psalmist has a word to say to a vast company.

Now just as we cannot speak with authority as to the nature of the handicap of this psalmist, no more can we do so with regard to many with whom we meet day by day. Of course, there are those whose handicaps are evident to all who know them. They have some physical defect or deformity that they cannot hide, or they may be battling with some hampering sickness that proclaims its presence to every seeing eye. Again it may be some mental or emotional quirk that is known only to a very few. Then there are those who so far as possible conceal their handicaps altogether. Sometimes they do so from pride. Sometimes they have a finer reason— they conceal their own wounds for the sake of others. They bear their burdens alone that others may be the more free. Therefore, they never speak of their handicaps except to God alone.

As we cannot know the nature of the affliction of the psalmist, no more can we say with authority why he was afflicted. It is generally assumed that his affliction was born of his own sin. Having wandered out of the way, the nettles have stung him and the thorns have pierced him. This, of course, is often the case. The ancient Hebrews had seen this happen so many times that they reached the conclusion that whenever any one suffered it was because of his own sin. That was the conviction of Job's friends. They could not account for his suffering on any other terms. "Who ever perished," they asked, "being innocent?" That also was the conviction of the disciples of Jesus. When they saw a certain blind man, their question was: "Who did sin, this man or his parents, that he was born blind?"

But while our own sin accounts for much of our suffering, it does not account for all of it. We cannot be sure that this psalmist was suffering as a direct result of his sin. He had gone astray, it is true. But his straying might have been in a most decent and respectable fashion. The blackout that came to him might have come at the hands of others. It might have come for reasons that he could not explain. For while there are tragedies that come into our lives for which we can find an intelligent reason, there are others that leave us perplexed and bewildered. Sometimes we can only cry with our Master, "My God, why?" But regardless of the nature of our handicaps and regardless of their cause, few of us get through life without experiencing one or more.

III

What did he do with his handicaps? What do we do? Our reactions are quite varied.

1. Some seek to ignore them. Now there may be some handicaps that are so insignificant that they can be safely ignored. But, generally speaking, such a course is a mistake. Whether a handicap is real or imaginary, it is better to face it. Often an imaginary handicap is more difficult than one

that is real. But always it is wise to face facts. I heard the head of a great business organization make this statement: "I have never known any man to go broke who knew where he stood at the close of each day." His declaration might not be universally true. But surely the man who faced the facts about his business would stand a better chance of success than the one who ignored the facts!

The truth is that we are not likely to cure many ills by simply looking in the other direction. If I see a small blaze on the floor of my home, I will not save my home from destruction by ignoring that blaze. Yet I have seen people afflicted with some physical handicap deliberately refuse to consult a physician lest he should tell them that their affliction was serious. How foolish! One cannot cure a cancer by merely ignoring it. The cancers that kill today are, generally speaking, those that were ignored either from ignorance or from fear. There are those who have defective hearing, but instead of facing the fact they expose themselves to constant embarrassments by trying to ignore it. What is even more common and quite as pathetic is to see some old body trying to carry on at seventy as if he were seventeen. We do not cure any of our ills by merely shutting our eyes.

2. This psalmist not only refused to ignore his affliction; he also refused to surrender to it. To surrender is quite as fatal as to ignore. There are those who go bravely forward until something trips them up. Then they fall flat and seemingly make no effort to rise again. Instead of bravely renewing the fight, they spend the remainder of their days wallowing in self-pity. Instead of fighting the best they can with their broken swords, they quit the battle and spend the remainder of their days telling how badly life has treated them

and how richly they deserve the devoted attention and pity of all their fellows.

Naturally, these have something to offer in the place of positive helpfulness. As a substitute, they tell what they would do but for their heavy handicaps. They tell how richly they would give if they were only as richly furnished as some of their fortunate friends. Meanwhile they forget that God does not ask any of us to use the resources of some gifted friend, but only those resources that are actually ours. He encourages us to do this by reminding us that he that is faithful in that which is least is faithful also in much. We honor the widow of the New Testament who immortalized herself by a single gift, not because of what she did with a billion dollars, but because of what she did with two mites.

3. Neither did this psalmist face his handicap in the spirit of a Stoic. There are those who pride themselves that they can stand up and take it. There is often a certain admirable courage about this type of character, but merely to stand up and take it is not enough. In fact, there are some things that we have to take whether we like them or not. There are those who battle their handicaps with a grim bitterness. These may develop a high degree of courage and pugnacity, but too often they become harsh and hard and sour.

4. Not only did this psalmist refuse to ignore his handicap; not only did he refuse either to surrender or merely to stand up and take it; he did something far better. He used it. As the ship uses the adverse wind to help it toward its desired haven, so he used his handicap to help him toward a fuller life. When a grain of sand gets into the shell of an oyster, sometimes that oyster merely stands up and takes it. At other times it does something far finer. It changes the wound that

the grain of sand makes into a pearl. Thus we can make our handicaps into helps.

IV

How can we use our handicaps?

1. We can make of them punching bags for the development of our own strength. Nearly all the progress that man has known has come because of his handicaps. Primitive man was a rather weak and helpless creature. Any fish could outswim him. Any bird could outfly him. Many of the animals were more fleet of foot than he, and many could defeat him in a combat. But he so used the handicap of weakness that today he can outswim the fish and outfly the eagle. Today he is really carrying out the primal command of God to have dominion. Of course, his tragedy is that he has often misused these great powers. Still he has changed his weakness into strength.

Years ago there was a small boy who suffered a severe burn. In fact, his legs were so badly burned that the physician looked at them and shook his head and said, "He will never walk again." But that boy refused to accept the verdict of that physician. He refused either to ignore or to surrender to his handicap. Instead, he so used his handicap that those burned legs enabled him to be one of the swiftest runners of all time. Glen Cunningham was doubtless the stronger every way because of his handicap.

I am thinking now of a minister who speaks with great freedom because he was never hampered by a manuscript or even by notes. How did he win this freedom? In his youth he longed to be a part of the debating society in his village school. But when he prepared notes for his speech, he shook so with fright that he could not hold them in his hand. He saw that he must either master what he was going to say or give up speaking altogether. Instead of yielding to his timidity, he used it. It has caused him to make careful preparation. It has also brought him to the place that any written helps would be worse than useless. Thus, he made a punching bag out of his handicap.

2. Not only can we use our handicaps for the strengthening of ourselves, but we can use them to strengthen and encourage others. When we meet one who has used his handicaps, such a one gives us courage. I am quite sure that Beethoven would have written wonderful music had his hearing been perfect. But by using his handicap, he doubtless produced greater music. Yet the fine courage of the man himself is even sweeter than his marvelous symphonies. Helen Keller would doubtless have shone under any circumstances, but through the wise use of her handicap she has come to a place of usefulness that she would perhaps never have attained without it.

Not only can we compel our handicaps to give us courage, but we can also compel them to give us an understanding heart. Who are the people that are of all others most helpful? Generally speaking, they are not those who have been born on the sunny side of the street. They are not those who have made the whole voyage of life over smooth seas. They are rather those who have known some kind of handicap. Thus, when life grows hard, men usually turn to those who have suffered—to those who have been educated in the hard school of adversity.

3. Finally we can use our handicaps by allowing them to convince us of our need of God and of our utter dependence

upon him. In our pride and self-sufficiency we tend eventually to cheat ourselves of what God is so eager to give. When days are sunny, we so often feel that we can somehow shift for ourselves. But when tragedy comes, we tend to die to our self-sufficiency. Of course, all of us need God however fortunate our circumstances! But we who are handicapped know that we must have him.

Now when we take our handicaps to him, he does one of two things for us—he either removes them or gives us grace to bear them. Paul had a handicap, a mysterious and torturing thorn. It was something that hampered him in his work, humiliated him in the eyes of the pagans whom he was seeking to win. Therefore, with eager confidence he took his handicap into the presence of God. He asked with persistent earnestness for its removal. But God refused to grant his request. Instead he did something far better. He said, "My grace is sufficient for thee: for my strength is made perfect in weakness." Thus Paul came to thank God for his thorn. Not only so, but millions who have read his story have come to join him in his paean of praise. Let your handicap bring you to God, and, whatever its nature, you too will come to thank God for it.

XIX

I'D PLAY TO WIN

*"Therefore let us also, seeing we are compassed about
with so great a cloud of witnesses, lay aside every weight,
and the sin which doth so easily beset us, and let us run
with patience the race that is set before us, looking unto
Jesus the author and perfecter of our faith."*

HEBREWS 12:1 (A.R.V.)

HERE IS A FIRST-CENTURY PREACHER SPEAKING TO A
group of fellow Christians who are finding their new
life beset by difficulties. In fact, they are so hard-pressed
that probably now and then some Pliable struggles out of the
Sea of Despond on the side next to the City of Destruction
and makes his way back home to tell all and sundry that the
adventure is so difficult that to undertake it will surely prove
futile. Others are looking over their shoulders at these re-
treating Pliables rather wistfully. They are wondering if
they, too, would not do well to give up the whole enterprise
and retreat to a safer and less dangerous position. It is to
hearten these wavering souls that the author speaks the brave
words of our text.

I

How does he seek to steady them? He makes no appeal to their cowardice or to their love of ease. Instead, he tells them with engaging candor that the good life is costly, that being a Christian is a serious and exacting business. In fact, to be a Christian is to be a spiritual athlete. Therefore, he takes his hearers out into the stadium and shows them the runners stripping for the race. "The Christian life," he said, "is a race to be run." He changes the figure: "It is a grim contest like that of two gladiators contending for the mastery. You cannot hope to win except at the price of struggle."

"In affirming the good, life will cost you something," he continues: "I am not claiming that your situation is unique. The life of faith has always been costly. The heroes of the faith of whom I have been speaking found it so. They were stoned; they were sawn asunder; they were slain with the sword; they wandered about in sheepskins and in goatskins, being destitute, afflicted, tormented (of whom the world was not worthy). They wandered in deserts and in the dens and caves of the earth. These lived grandly because they dared to pay the price for such living."

In thus speaking of the Christian life as a race to be run, as a strenuous game to be played, as a battle to be fought, the author is speaking in harmony with the New Testament as a whole. John, the author of Revelation, pictures the life of the saint as one that clashes with conflict. When he gives us a glimpse at those who have won, he tells us that they came up out of great tribulation. When he tells us how they won, he makes it plain that their victory was due to the fact that they did not count their lives as dear unto themselves. He constantly pictures the business of being a Christian as an earnest and costly business.

Paul also speaks to the same purpose. He was thrown much with soldiers. His language is saturated with the spirit of the stadium and the spirit of the battlefield. Now he is in the ring: "So fight I not as one that beateth the air." Again he is on the race track: "I therefore so run, not as uncertainly —I have finished my course." Again he is on the field of battle. "Put on the complete armor of God, so that you may be able to stand your ground in the evil day, and, having fought to the end, to remain victors on the field."

How did these saints come by their conviction that to be a Christian involved conflict? They learned it in part through their own experiences and through the experiences of their fellow saints. Above all else, they had learned it from their Master. Jesus never uttered a single word that could appeal to our cowardice and softness. When one asked him, "Are there few that be saved?" he did not answer as to whether there would be few or many. He rather said, "Strive to enter in." Strive as in a game. Struggle as in a battle. Agonize as he himself agonized in Gethsemane. "For many will seek to enter and shall not be able." They shall not be able, not because entrance is impossible, but because they were not willing to pay the price. "Therefore," says this author, "if you mean to win this game, if you expect to come out victor in this race, you must be prepared to give your best."

II

How, then, are we to run so as to win? In plain common sense, we are to divest ourselves of all handicaps. What are some of the handicaps that we are to refuse?

1. If we are to run successfully, we must avoid the handicap of positive sin. We must give up every known wrong. This we are to do because sin separates us from God and is therefore weakening. There is nothing that clips the thews of our strength, there is nothing that so slows us down as wrong-doing. While Samson remained loyal to the will of God, he was unconquerable. But when he broke his vow and became disloyal, he was as weak as any other man. Sin always issues in weakness. It is only right that is truly strong

> "My good blade carves the casques of men,
> My tough lance thrusteth sure,
> My strength is as the strength of ten,
> Because my heart is pure."

2. Not only must we lay aside every sin but also every weight. There are certain practices and pastimes, innocent in themselves, that become weights because we use them in such a fashion as to allow them to slow us down. A minister once asked me if I preached against bridge. "No," I replied, "some of my people play. If I preached against it, I would give it more attention than it deserves. Besides," I continued, "I don't feel that it would be wise to turn my guns loose on a field mouse when I am surrounded by so many roaring lions." Yet bridge, mumblety-peg, or any other game may become a weight and a positive sin if we take it off the side line and put it onto the main line.

Here is the sanest possible test of those pastimes and recreations in which a Christian may indulge. As Christians we are out to win the race. We are bent on playing the game successfully. Everything is to be made to bend to this one purpose. Whatever helps, we are to take on; whatever hinders, we are to throw away, however innocent that something might be in itself. If I am a member of the athletic squad, for me to eat sweets or to smoke cigarettes is to sin against my team, provided such practices lessen my efficiency as an athlete.

As a boy I had to cross the Buffalo River every day on my way to school. One morning as I was fording the river, I noticed a crow that was wading about in the shallow water seeking for food. As I came near, the crow rose and flew; but to my surprise he came to earth after a flight of only a few yards. At his next effort he flew a yet shorter distance. At last I was able to catch that crow with my hands. Why was this the case? The crow was not wounded. Nobody had broken or clipped his wings. This was the matter: that crow had slipped his toe into the shell of a mussel, and that mussel had closed down upon it. Therefore it was burdened by an extra weight. That weight did not kill the crow. But, in spite of that fact, the weight so hampered him as to cause him to fall into the hand of an enemy.

There was a farmer in my native state who, with a small shotgun, killed a great American eagle. The farmer was amazed that he was able to get near enough to him to kill him with such a gun. This bird was a magnificent creature measuring seven feet from tip to tip. When he examined him, however, he found that an old steel trap was clinging to one of his legs. Months, perhaps even years before, someone had set a trap for the great bird and had caught him. But the eagle broke away, taking the trap with him. The trap did not kill him, but it so lowered his efficiency that he became an easy prey for his deadly foe. In this race we must throw away every handicap.

3. Not only must we refuse to handicap ourselves by posi-

tive sin and by needless weights, but we are to refuse to handicap ourselves by neglecting those helps that will make us more efficient. When the war broke out, we were heavily handicapped because our soldiers were not trained and because we were not provided with the munitions of war. The soldier who goes into battle without training and equipment labors under a heavy handicap. The Christian soldier who goes into battle without the resources that God has provided for him also labors under a handicap.

III

What are some of the helps that, according to this author, we are to use if we are to run the race at our best.

1. There is the forward look. He reminds us that this is a race set before us. That sounds a bit trite I know. But in reality it is not. We cannot hope to win this race by merely running in circles. We cannot hope to win with our eyes turned backward. In a notable football game a few years ago a capable player got possession of the ball and made a run of seventy yards. It was a brilliant performance except for one reason—he was running in the wrong direction. He was running backward toward the enemy's goal instead of toward his own. We can hope to run well only so long as we keep the forward look.

2. We are to run in the realization that we are a part of a great team. We are not out to play our game or to run our race alone. There are all about us those who see our visions and dream our dreams. The fact that these touch elbows with us hearten us and give us courage. We are part of a great company. Some of them fight at our side today. Others have passed within the veil. But these have not lost interest in the

fight. They are the old varsity graduates of other years that have themselves mightily won and are watching with eager interest while we play our part.

Not only do our fellow Christians here and yonder hearten us for the conflict by their presence and their sympathy, but they bear their testimony to the reality and worth of the prize for which we run. That is what the author has in mind when he says, "Therefore let us also, seeing we are compassed about with so great a cloud of witnesses run." These are not witnesses simply in that they are spectators, but they are rather witnesses in that they give their testimony to the reality and worth of the prizes for which we run. We are to run, therefore, heartened by the fact that we are not alone, and remembering that the prize is very real and of infinite worth.

3. Finally, we are to run with patience—that is, patient endurance. This race is not a hundred-yard dash. It is a cross-country run. The track stretches away to the sunset. Therefore, we need persistence. We must guard against what is perhaps the greatest peril of the Christian life, the peril of fainting. "In due season," declares Paul, "we shall reap if we faint not." If we lack the grit and grace to persist, no power on earth or in heaven can give us victory. But if we have the grit and grace to persist, nothing in earth or hell can defeat us.

IV

How, then, shall we get this persistence that spells victory?

1. By looking to Jesus as the author, the captain, the way-shower. We are to look to our Lord as an example of the way this race ought to be run. How did he run it?

(1) He ran with his eye fixed on the goal. What was his goal? It was the joy set before him, the joy of perfect conformity to the will of God, the joy of yielding completely to that yoke which he himself declared was kindly. It was the joy also of victory, not only for himself but for others. The goal that he kept before his eyes was the joy of a world redeemed.

(2) Fixing his eyes thus on the goal, he ran even though his running was costly. He ran in the face of opposition. Since he met opposition, you and I may expect to meet it. Some of these saints felt that the fact that they were suffering was an indication of God's indifference. This writer declares that it is rather the mark of God's love and of their sonship. If the road you are traveling is altogether easy, you had better examine your guidepost, for the road of vital Christian living is a road beset by difficulties.

(3) Not only did Jesus run in the face of opposition, but he ran in spite of it. The goal to which he looked was so alluring that he endured the cross, looking with contempt upon its shame. That is, he ran, though it caused him to pay the last full measure of devotion. "You," says the author, "have not gone that far yet. 'Ye have not yet resisted unto blood, striving against sin.' But this you must be willing to do." "It is enough for the disciple that he be as his master."

(4) Running thus in spite of opposition, with his eye fixed on the goal, he won. And God has given him a name that is above every name. He has now "sat down on the right hand of the Majesty on high." When we run as he ran, we too may win.

2. We are to look to Jesus, not only as our example, but as the perfecter of faith. We are to look to him as our perfecter,

as our friend, and as our helper. The word here used for "looking" is to look away from all else. We are to look away from our handicaps, to look away from ourselves, to Jesus, who is able to supply our every need. Do you remember that night of storm when the disciples were desperately manning the oars of their little vessel and yet getting nowhere? They look up to see Jesus coming to them across the waters. At first, thinking that he was a ghost, they cried out for fear. Then came that quieting word, "It is I; be not afraid."

Then Simon turned instantly from cowardice to courage. "Lord, if it be thou, bid me come to thee on the water." He now is ready to dare the impossible. "Come," was the simple reply of Jesus. Then what? Simon climbed down out of the vessel and walked on the water. He looked away from everything else to his Master, and while he thus looked he won. But when he fixed his eyes on his difficulties, at once he began to sink. If we are to run victoriously, we must run looking unto Jesus.

A short time ago a young fellow, Gilbert Dodds by name, ran the fastest mile, so far as the record goes, that was ever run. More than thirteen thousand people applauded his triumph. When he was asked to tell those thousands in the open-air stadium and those far greater thousands that were listening over the radio the secret of his victory, he answered in simple sincerity, "I asked God to help me every step that I took." That is, this young chap in running his race, ran looking unto Him who is the source of all power. It is his conviction that there came to him a strength as he thus ran that could not have come in any other fashion.

I know how the wise will smile cynically at the thought of God helping to run a race. In those days when the Kentucky

Colonels were winning one triumph after another in football, the team used to go into a huddle for prayer as soon as they ran onto the field. When a newspaperman asked cynically, "Do you mean that you asked God to take the victory from your opponents and give it to you?" The captain answered, "No, we do not pray to win. We pray to play. We ask God to give us the grit and stamina to play the game as it ought to be played." So, I am sure, Gilbert Dodds prayed. Thus praying, he was able to run at his best. Thus looking unto Jesus, we shall run our best. "Look unto me," he invites, "and be ye saved, all the ends of the earth."

DATE DUE

HIGHSMITH 45-102   PRINTED IN U.S.A.